A Literary Journey to Jewish Identity

Re-Reading Bellow, Roth, Malamud, Ozick, and Other Great Jewish Writers

By Stephen B. Shepard

For Bernie,
To life and literature,
on your 90th !
Best wishes,

Steve Shepard

For information, please contact: stephenshepard5@gmail.com

ISBN paperback: 978-0-9892133-8-7
ISBN e-book: 978-0-9892133-7-0

Cover and interior design by Malcolm Frouman.

Credit for author photograph on back cover:
CUNY Graduate School of Journalism.

LIBRARY OF CONGRESS CATALOGING-IN-PUBLICATION DATA

Shepard, Stephen B
.

Some of the material in Chapter 2 first appeared in
Deadlines & Disruption: My Turbulent Path From Print to Digital, published by
McGraw-Hill in 2012 © by Stephen B. Shepard.

First Edition.

Bayberry
books

In memory of my parents,
Ruth and William Shepard,
and my sister,
Barbara Glaser.

Contents

Prologue   9

CHAPTER 1
What's He Gonna do, Open a History Store?   12

CHAPTER 2
My Jewish Awakening   17

CHAPTER 3
Jew vs. Jew: Philip Roth's *Eli, The Fanatic*   31

CHAPTER 4
Gansevoort Street: The World of *Our* Fathers   39

CHAPTER 5
Is Willy Loman Jewish? Does It Matter?   53

CHAPTER 6
My Encounter With Isaac Bashevis Singer   61

CHAPTER 7
The Immigrants From Kolomaya   70

CHAPTER 8
Eight Guys Reading Saul Bellow   77

CHAPTER 9

Literary Anti-Semitism   94

CHAPTER 10

Philip Roth's Turning Point   98

CHAPTER 11

Bernard Malamud: The Forgotten Man   114

CHAPTER 12

Greenhorns and Yankees   132

CHAPTER 13

The Jewish John Updike   136

CHAPTER 14

Cynthia Ozick: Keeper of the Flame   148

CHAPTER 15

"Who Owns Anne Frank?"   160

CHAPTER 16

What Kind of Jew Am I?   167

Epilogue   178

Notes   181
Acknowledgments   196
About the Author   198
Index   199

"So we beat on, boats against the current,
borne ceaselessly into the past."

– *F. Scott Fitzgerald*

"What's he gonna do, open a history store?"

– *Ruth Shepard*

Prologue

I never thought of myself as particularly interested in things Jewish, or that I possessed anything that might be called a Jewish identity. I was Jewish, for sure, but I rarely dwelt on what it meant. I stopped observing Jewish rituals not long after my Bar Mitzvah, and my first wife wasn't Jewish. I simply retreated into my own private diaspora: a Jew in name only, a non-religious member of the tribe, linked only tenuously to the heritage, culture, and social values of Judaism. I had left the fold – not to return for several years.

Yet I was aware, especially during my formative years in the 1950s and 1960s, that there was a flowering of the Jewish-American novel, and that many of the writers I was reading were Jewish. Some of these writers were overtly Jewish, like Bernard Malamud and Philip Roth; some were slyly so, like Saul Bellow; and some were not-at all-so, like J.D. Salinger[1] and Norman Mailer. What, I wondered, did it mean to be a Jewish-American writer? Was there such a thing as a Jewish-American novel? And even more basic: Why did I care so much about these books?

In fact, it was largely my interest in these Jewish writers that allowed my Jewish identity to flicker at all during my days of absence from Judaism. I read about Jewish characters and concerns, absorbed the lessons of immigration and assimilation, felt the many ways of being Jewish. There were times I exalted these writers as heroes, as if they were baseball stars. Even if Holden Caulfield went to a prep school, even if *The Naked and the Dead* was just a war novel, I took a certain pride in knowing their creators were Jews who could write about anything.

Jewish fiction often touched me more than all the ritual I observed at home and all the prayers I sat though in my parents' Orthodox synagogue in the Bronx. Some stories made me uncomfortable, as in the suffering depicted by Malamud or the father-son tension in some plays by Arthur Miller. Other stories seemed to speak directly to me about what it means to be Jewish, as in much early Roth fiction. For secular Jews like us, says my friend Sam Norich, the president of *The Forward*, a 120-year-old Jewish publication: "Literature is our liturgy. It's the way we identify."

In re-reading many of these authors – and books about them – I learned many things. I was dismayed by the anti-Semitism directed at Bellow by some of our best-known WASP writers. I was fascinated by what I found out about the literary feud between Malamud and Roth over the nature of Jewishness. I was intrigued that it took 50 years for Miller to acknowledge that Willy Loman, the famous Everyman in *Death of a Salesman*, was actually a Jewish character. I rediscovered the "Jewish" novels of John Updike, that quintessential Protestant, and the questions he implicitly raised about Jewish identity. And in re-visiting the work of Cynthia Ozick, I found myself contemplating anew the Holocaust: how remembrance became for me a key part of what it means to be Jewish.

I'm not attempting a scholarly critique of Jewish-American literature. Rather, I want to describe my encounters with a few writers who inspired me, who influenced my Jewishness, and whose books often stayed in my memory for years. I write as an enthusiastic reader, a fan watching his team play. My sense of Jewish identity has ebbed and flowed over the years. I am now a proud member of the ancient faith, but I still have questions, still want to argue about it. I suppose that too is a very Jewish thing – and I'm grateful that the Jewish writers in post-war America helped me find my way, my place in the Jewish firmament.

ONE

"What's He Gonna Do, Open a History Store?"

If I had it to do over again, I would major in English in college – instead of the engineering I did study. But at 16, when I graduated from the Bronx High School of Science, I was simply too immature to realize that college was about more than just preparing for a profession. "What do you want to be when you grow up?" The answer in my immigrant milieu was always: doctor, lawyer, engineer, or teacher. Once, I remember telling my parents that a friend had dropped out of the engineering school at City College to major in history. My mother's instant response: "What's he gonna do, open a history store?"

Now that retirement has given me something of a second chance, I've started reading in earnest. Not just plowing through a revered novel, but reading it carefully, taking notes, checking out the reviews and critical commentary. I'm trying to read, or perhaps re-read with new understanding, all those books that define the literary canon – the very books that played second fiddle to all the math and physics I stud-ied in school. Many of these books, it turns out, are by the Jewish-American writers who dominated American literature during the post-war period.

It's hard to define Jewish-American literature or character-ize a Jewish-American writer, and many writers who happen to be Jewish have long hated these labels. Saul Bellow once lamented that being called a Jewish writer is rather like being called "an Eskimo cellist...".[1] But the fact remains that most of the heavyweights of the time (with plenty of exceptions) were Jewish – from Mailer, Salinger, and E.L. Doctorow to the cele-brated trio of Bellow, Malamud, and Roth. It was Joseph Hell-er who brought "Catch 22" to the American idiom and Arthur Miller who told us that attention must be paid to America's everyman, Willy Loman.

What, if anything, did these writers have in common? Is there something particularly Jewish in a book written by a Jew? Often there is. Sometimes it's in the characters, like Mor-ris Bober in Malamud's *The Assistant*. Sometimes it's the family, like the Portnoys or the Patimkins in Roth's fiction. Some-times it's the theme of alienation or otherness, as in Bellow's *The Victim* or *Herzog*. Sometimes, it's the clash of cultures – of immigrants in the vastness of America, as in Isaac Bashevis Singer's *Enemies, A Love Story*. Sometimes it's the humor, as in a Grace Paley story. Sometimes it's the liturgical, as in almost everything by Cynthia Ozick.

And sometimes it's the sensibility – what Roth describes as "the nervousness, the excitability, the arguing, the drama-tizing, the indignation, the obsessiveness, the touchiness, the playacting – above all the *talking*. The talking and the shouting...It isn't what it's talking *about* that makes a book Jewish – it's that the book won't shut up...won't leave you alone." [2]

As a fan, I had a fairly complete collection of first editions of these books, many of them signed. I started rereading some of these favorites even before I stepped down as dean of the CUNY Journalism School. But once I had more time, I decided to go back even further, to read the Jewish immigrant writers from earlier in the 20th century. I told myself I was looking for precedent: how the earlier writers laid the groundwork for the post-war golden age. But I think I was also searching for my own roots, what Irving Howe called the *World of Our Fathers*.[3] Or perhaps the world of my father, who grew up on the Lower East Side of New York and worked on Gansevoort Street when it really was a meat-packing district.

I had long ago read Henry Roth's extraordinary book, *Call It Sleep*, which was published in 1934, when Roth was 28. Now I re-read it, moved more than I had remembered by the plight of the immigrant boy on the Lower East Side. Like many others, I felt the pain of David Schearle, the frightened Jewish kid from a turbulent family trying to negotiate his way at home and in the streets.

I was especially intrigued by the story of Henry Roth himself and how his great book vanished from public awareness for 30 years. Roth disappeared along with his book and was said to be living on a duck farm in Maine, suffering from colossal writer's block. Then in 1964, after some literary lobbying by Alfred Kazin and Leslie Fiedler, Avon Books issued a paperback, which was lauded by Irving Howe on the front page of *The New York Times Book Review* as a lost masterpiece ("one of the few genuinely distinguished novels written by a 20th century American").[4] It was as if a great archeological find had been unearthed. In short order, more than a million copies of the paperback were sold.

Henry Roth finally resurfaced as a novelist in the 1990s with a quartet of linked books collectively called *Mercy of a Rude Stream*, which picked up where *Call It Sleep* left off in telling the story of Roth's young protagonist.[5] The books were treated mostly as a curiosity – an occasion for the retelling of Roth's own personal odyssey – a story "mummified into legend," in the words of Roth's biographer, Steven G. Kellman.[6] Only this time there was a major revelation: in both fiction and fact, Roth confessed that he had a long incestuous liaison with his sister, Rose, starting when he was a teenager. It was the shame of that relationship, we were told, which largely explained Roth's long literary hibernation. Roth's admission of his incest apparently unburdened him enough that he was able to write *Mercy of a Rude Stream*. He died in 1995 at age 89. One final novel was published after his death, *An American Type*, but it had little of the old magic.

Next up for me was Abraham Cahan, who wrote in 1917 one of the most seminal novels of the Jewish immigrant period: *The Rise of David Levinsky*. It is the saga of a penniless immigrant making it big in America – and the devastating price he paid for his greenhorn-to-Yankee assimilation. An anonymous reviewer in *The New York Times* gave it a favorable notice in 1917, though the review now sounds condescending (it refers to "...certain members of the race...").[7]

When a paperback was issued nearly a half century later, it was reviewed in *The Times* by none other than Saul Bellow. He called Cahan a "gifted writer" who was "psychologically shrewd" and avoided the easy sentimentality that plagued other immigrant stories. Nonetheless, Bellow concluded that the "book is more interesting as social history than literature."[8] Bellow went on to win a Nobel Prize in Literature, so to quarrel with his judgment risks sounding like a greenhorn myself. But I have to admit I was moved by the story and found the writing more than serviceable. (Cahan also founded the *Jewish Daily Forward*, which is still published as *The Forward*, in Yiddish as well as English.) I so enjoyed reading the novel that I splurged on a first edition complete with the rare dust jacket. I felt as if I were holding history in my hands.

I sampled some other immigrant fare, including *Bread Givers*, a novel written in 1925 by Anzia Yezierska, which tells a similar saga of striving, but this time of a poor Jewish girl who rejects the traditional role dictated for women by religious strictures and cultural norms. The story is rife with hardship and struggle, a tale of tenements and sweatshops, but ultimately the heroine prevails on her own in her own way.

Similar books with the same themes have been written about other immigrant groups – the Irish, of course, but also the Italians, the Chinese, the Hispanics, and many others. It is a particularly American genre. But to read of one's own roots, so rich in time, place, and lore, is especially resonant.

I had finally opened the history store that my mother had joked about.

TWO

My Jewish Awakening

I soon realized that my interest in Jewish literature, my quest for roots, was really a search for meaning, especially now that my working life was over. Some people my age talk pompously about their "legacy," suggesting a gift to mankind, rather like Aunt Agnes leaving money to the Smithsonian. Whatever word we use, we're all talking about the same thing: What did my life add up to, for better or worse? Did I have any lasting affect? Did I matter?

The quest for meaning presses in as we get older. And for me, it means coming to terms with being Jewish. Why else was I so interested in Jewish-American writers? But I hadn't thought about my Jewishness in any deep way, perhaps because the whole idea was fraught with ambivalence in my family.

Some early memories come to mind. On Rosh Hashonah and Yom Kippur, the major holidays, I walked with my father, William Shepard, to our local synagogue in the Bronx, an Orthodox *shul* called Kingsbridge Heights Jewish Center, and sat with him for some of the service. Most of the neighborhood men who made the same trek carried their *talis* (prayer shawl) in a nice velvet prayer bag embossed with the six-sided Star of David. Not my father. He carried this sacred cloth in a plain manila envelope. When I asked why, I never got a satisfactory answer.

I sometimes felt he didn't want to be publicly identified as a Jew. But why? He always showed respect for the religion, as well as pride in Jewish accomplishment. Yet, in some ways, he gave off signs of fear, as if a declaration of his Jewishness would make him a marked man – a victim of the persecution his parents faced in Europe, or the discrimination he felt in his ghetto-like youth on the Lower East Side, or the difficulty a man named William Shapiro faced in the job market. Better to keep it quiet, change your name, don't make waves.

There was another holiday ritual, which I've come to call "the parable of the Yom Kippur nickel." My father was keenly interested in the news, especially politics and sports, and he read three newspapers a day: the *New York Times*, the *New York Herald Tribune*, and the *New York Post*. The news was so important to him that on Yom Kippur, the Day of Atonement, when he fasted and spent the entire day in our synagogue, he gave me a nickel (the only money he carried on this strict holiday) and told me to go to Kingsbridge Road to buy the *Times* and take it home for him to read that night. He told me to put the paper under my jacket so no one would know I had committed an act of commerce on the holiest day of the year.

As these recollections suggest, our family's attitude toward

Jewishness turned out to be highly complicated. When my grandmother (my mother's mother) was alive and living in our apartment building, she and my mother often spoke Yiddish together, especially when they didn't want me to understand what they were saying. My mother called it "speaking Jewish." We kept a kosher home, which not only meant special food, but also separate dishes for meat and dairy meals. Yet after my grandmother's death when I was 10, the kosher practices gradually ended, and ultimately there was even bacon in my mother's kitchen.

Like many immigrants, my mother, Ruth Tanner Shepard, was deeply conflicted about the old world versus the new, the nostalgic ties to her mother's very Jewish life versus her own drive to be Americanized. She often told the story of her mother going to the fishmonger every Friday morning to buy carp or flounder for the *Shabbos* dinner. To keep the fish fresh, my grandmother filled the bathtub with cold water and let the fish swim until it was time for the ritual slaughter: a tender bop over the head with a rolling pin, removal of the head, tail, and gills, and then into the oven.

I never knew whether my mother's story was of the "old country," as she called it, or the Jewish neighborhood on East 114th Street in Manhattan, where she grew up. In any case, it was no longer her world. We lived in the Bronx, immigrant heaven, and there were no fish swimming in the bathtub. But it was her history, and she told the story with evident pride and warmth. She just didn't want to live that life. She wanted to be "modern," as she often put it – and that to her meant shedding some of her Orthodox Jewish identity.

My father's side had its own anxieties about religion. One of my father's older brothers had married a German Jew, who thought of herself as a higher caste than the peasant Jews who had emigrated from Poland, like my father's family. Those fancier-than-thou pretensions led her to urge my uncle to change the family name from Shapiro to Shepard. My father, nudged by my mother, followed suit in 1937. My sister, born in 1936, was thus a Shapiro at birth. I, born in 1939, was a Shepard.

As a result of this schism, there were two wings in my father's family, the more-traditional Shapiros and the more Americanized Shepards. Neither of my parents spoke about the old world of European ghettos that had spawned their families – an unacknowledged policy of don't ask, don't tell. They wanted nothing to do with Poland, and they pleaded ignorance whenever I raised questions. They desperately wanted to be American.

A lot of this was understandable. There was, after all, much discrimination against Jews – restricted neighborhoods, off-limit jobs, and quotas at some colleges. It was not lost on me that my Uncle Lou, my mother's brother, had earned a Master's degree from MIT in 1924, but couldn't get a job in private industry, it was often said, because he was Jewish. To be Jewish, I came to understand, was to be a victim.

And, of course, the horror of the Holocaust. I vividly remember, at age six or so, seeing the photographs of the newly liberated concentration camps in *Life* magazine, that pre-television chronicle of the world in black and white. There were pictures of the dead, their emaciated bodies stacked like so many cords of wood. And of the survivors, on the brink of death, hollowed-out shells of humanity staring back at all of us, as if to ask: How did this happen? [1] Even families, like mine, that were not direct victims of the Holocaust were traumatized by it. In my home, to be Jewish in that era was to be scared and vulnerable.

And less religious. When I was eight or so, my Aunt Anna, my mother's sister, shocked everyone at a family dinner when she announced that she no longer believed in God. If God really existed, she asked, why did He allow the Jews to be slaughtered? To an eight-year-old boy, it was a very good question.

In the early 1950s, at the height of the McCarthy-era hysteria, Julius and Ethel Rosenberg were arrested for spying for the Soviet Union. My parents were very upset. How could Jews do such a thing? And wouldn't we all be blamed? I remember discussing this with my mother when I was 13, around the time the Rosenbergs were executed for treason. The conversation went something like this:

13-year-old boy: "Why are you so upset about the Rosenbergs?"

Jewish Mother: "Because they are Jewish."

13-year-old boy: "So what?"

Jewish Mother: "It's not good for us."

13-year-old boy: "We didn't do anything wrong. Just because the Rosenbergs are Jewish, doesn't have anything to do with us."

Jewish Mother: "You don't understand."

I didn't. But just a few years after the Holocaust, the fear came through. Yes, I should stay out of trouble, be a good boy. But her history had taught her that Jews would be blamed even when they didn't do anything wrong. The message I took away: Don't stand out as a Jew. Be a Shepard not a Shapiro. Assimilation became a form of disguise for me, a way of escaping the victimization I saw as inevitable.

Is there such a thing as a lapsed Jew, like a lapsed Catholic? If so, I became one. My religious ambivalence, born of anxiety, no doubt laid the groundwork for me to marry someone who wasn't Jewish – in effect, giving me permission to marry a *shiksa*. And so I did.

I met my first wife, Susan, when we were both young writers at *Business Week* in the mid 1960s – she writing about economics and I about technology. A native of suburban Chicago and a graduate of Radcliffe College, Susan lived in Greenwich Village with two Cliffie roommates. I suppose all *shiksa* fantasies are alike in their assimilationist urges, but in my version there was no blond goddess. Susan had dark eyes with dark hair parted in the middle. I have to admit, with much retrospective embarrassment, that I was attracted to the idea of dating a WASP from Radcliffe. To an intellectually aspiring kid, what could be more American? What could be more Shepard and less Shapiro?

It soon got serious. But a big problem loomed. Susan's mother immediately made it abundantly clear, mostly in bitter, alcohol-fueled letters, that she opposed her daughter marrying a Jew. It was a terrible blow for Susan. Her mother, a retired school teacher, had raised Susan and her sister, Joann, by herself, ever since her divorce when Susan was in the fifth grade. I had never experienced such overt anti-Semitism. Rather than getting angry at her mother for her bigotry or ashamed over my own social climbing, I was mostly numb. How could an educated woman, a schoolteacher no less, be an anti-Semite in this day and age? As naïve as it seems, I couldn't fathom that someone would object to me, without meeting me, simply because I was Jewish. I was more worried about my own parents' reaction to my marrying out of the ancient faith. They weren't thrilled at the idea, but they met Susan, liked her, and decided not to make a fuss.

And so, after living together in my brownstone apartment on West 75th Street, we were married on November 4, 1967 – at the Harvard Club, natch. Her mother did not attend the wedding. Four months later, we moved to London, where I would be a correspondent for *Business Week* and Susan would freelance and take courses.

In the early 1970s, after we returned from London and Susan was finishing law school at Columbia, she and her mother ended their six-year estrangement. I went to Chicago with Susan to visit her mother, Helen, chaperoned by Susan's younger sister, Joann, and Joann's husband. Helen was cordial, and so was I, but not a word was said about her earlier behavior, as if nothing had ever happened. If Susan wanted to reconcile with her mother, I would go along. A couple of years later, Helen contracted liver cancer and came to New York for treatment at Memorial Sloan-Kettering Cancer Center. She stayed with us for a few weeks at our apartment on West 79th Street, and I sometimes escorted her to her doctor appointments. She returned home for further treatment in Chicago, but died a year or so later. She never apologized for her behavior, and I never asked her about it.

My marriage to Susan was rocky pretty much from the start, but I never knew how much to attribute to her mother's rejection of her and me. Religion was rarely an issue for the two of us. Neither one of us was observant, and the only religious tension I can recall occurred at Christmas time, when Susan wanted a Christmas tree. We usually got one, but I never felt comfortable with it in the house. Religion might have reared its problematic head more explicitly if we had children − or even discussed having them. But both of us sensed our marriage wouldn't last. Sure enough, soon after I took a job at *Newsweek* as a senior editor in 1976, we broke up. After the difficult moment of telling my parents that we were getting a divorce, I found myself eerily relieved. Not calm or joyful, just relieved. And ready to start anew.

Susan later remarried, had two children, and built a successful career as a lawyer. She called to express condolences when my father died, but there's been radio silence for more than 30 years. The ocean waves have long since washed away our sand castle.

After we split, it didn't take more than a microsecond to entertain thoughts of my *Newsweek* colleague, Lynn Povich, who also was recently divorced. She was striking, with piercing blue eyes and close-cropped hair that had silver tinges, even in her early 30s. There we were, two senior editors, friends as well as colleagues − in the same place, at the same time, in the same situation. And both Jewish − no small thing considering my first marriage. Surely this was meant to be, a clear case of manifest destiny – or *bashert*, as my mother would later say. We have been together for 40 years, and counting.

Lynn, who grew up in Washington, joined *Newsweek* in 1965, fresh out of Vassar, as a secretary in the magazine's Paris bureau. Within a couple of years, she had transferred to New York, first as a researcher – treading the obligatory career path for women. She worked her way up, doing lifestyle stories, including fashion, and soon became one of the few women writers in *Newsweek*'s history (or *Time*'s). She always said it was a fluke because none of the men wanted to write about fashion.

In the late 1960s, a group of women, including Lynn, began secretly meeting to discuss the obvious inequity that all the researchers were women and all the writers (except Lynn) were men. By 1970, 46 *Newsweek* women (Lynn among the ringleaders) sued the magazine for gender discrimination, the first and most significant such case in the media world and the forerunner of many others, including at *Time* and the *New York Times*. Ultimately, the two sides settled, laying the groundwork for gender integration at *Newsweek* and elsewhere in the media world. In 1975, when he became editor, Ed Kosner appointed Lynn as the first woman senior editor in the magazine's history. Lynn told the whole story in her 2012 book, *The Good Girls Revolt*,[2] which was made into a television series by Amazon in 2016.

And what of Lynn's roots? Her mother, Ethyl Friedman Povich, was born in Radom, Poland, but was raised in Washington, then a segregated, rather Southern city. (JFK joked it was a "town of Northern charm and Southern efficiency.") Soft-spoken and pretty, Ethyl was a stay-at-home Mom, like my own mother – both women typical of their generation. Lynn's father was Shirley Povich, the well-known, elegant sports writer for the *Washington Post*, whose career at the time I met him had already spanned more than 50 years.[3]

Shirley's odyssey was family legend. His own father ran a furniture store in the wealthy summer enclave of Bar Harbor, Maine, an odd place for an Orthodox Jewish family, and Shirley and his eight siblings lived over the family store. During the summer, when the millionaires came to their "cottages," Shirley caddied at the local golf club, where one of his regulars was Edward B. McLean, who just happened to own the *Washington Post*. When Shirley was finishing high school, Mr. McLean offered him a job at the *Post*. He hitched a ride to Boston, slept on a bench in Boston Commons, then took a boat to New York and a train to Washington. He started at the *Post* in 1922, age 17, as a copy boy, was promoted to cub reporter on the police beat, then switched to sports. He ultimately became one of the nation's premier sports columnists, a dapper gentlemen in a Fedora, writing six columns a week for decades. He wrote his last column on the day before he died, at nearly 93, in 1998.

Soon after Lynn and I started dating, I was eager to introduce her to my parents, who had retired to Florida, and we had a chance when they came to New York for a visit. Over dinner, Lynn told them about her family, her mother's immigrant roots and her father's saga – his Lithuanian *shtetl* parents, his early years in Bar Harbor, his remarkable career at the *Washington Post*. Then, quite casually, she asked them about their own family backgrounds. I held my breath. Never had they talked about what they still regarded as the Old World, always disclaiming any knowledge of European ghettos. This time, surely encouraged by Lynn's pride in her family heritage and her deep feelings for Judaism, they each blurted out the names of long-forgotten *shtetls*, both in present-day Poland. Stunned, I quickly wrote down the names: Suwalki for my father's family, Kolomaya for my mother's.[4] Lynn, an observant Jew, had broken through my parents repression of their past.

A couple of years later, at the Diaspora Museum in Tel Aviv, I avidly read the history of these villages, which had been wiped out by the Nazis. I didn't hear the name Kolomaya again until recently, when two of my cousins, Marilyn Tanner Oettinger and Sandy Sternlicht, mentioned it while I was preparing our family tree. I was coming full circle.

My Jewish identity snapped into focus on my first trip to Germany. Though I had lived in London and traveled through much of Europe, I had never been to Germany until I went as the editor of *Business Week* in 1986. With Berlin still divided between East and West, our bureau was located in Bonn, a sleepy village promoted to world capital during the Cold War. The bureau chief was a former colleague from New York, a delightful Texan named Jack Pluenneke, who accompanied me everywhere. We took the wonderful two-hour train ride along the Rhine, from Bonn to Frankfurt, the financial capital of Germany. We interviewed politicians and businessmen. We toured a Volkswagen plant. And then we went to Berlin.

Suddenly, the East-West tensions that dominated postwar Germany didn't seem to matter. All I could think about was Berlin's Nazi past. The first frisson occurred when I saw, quite inadvertently, the changing of the guard in front of some German building – a routine occurrence without the pomp of a similar ceremony at Buckingham Palace. Yet the Prussian guards marched in goose step, and I was frozen in a kind of anachronistic chill. We moved on, and I didn't say anything to Jack.

The next day, Jack asked if I would like to visit an old Jewish cemetery we were about to drive by in East Berlin. We got out of the car and walked around the unkempt cemetery for about 20 minutes. The tombstones, some lying on the ground, had the usual German-Jewish names. Some of them dated to the 19th century, and there were plenty from the 1920s and early 1930s. But there was nothing after 1933, not one tombstone. It was hardly a revelation that normal Jewish life ended in Germany after 1933, but I was stunned by the emotional impact I felt.

A day or two later, riding around Berlin, I noticed a vacant lot surrounded by a chain-link fence in an otherwise built-up area, like a parcel of land awaiting development in New York. It had a large mound near the center. "What's that?" I asked. "Oh," came the nonchalant reply from our driver, "that's where Hitler's bunker was."

There it was, Hitler's command center in the final days of the war, the underground capital of Evil, the very heart of anti-Semitism. That's where he lived! That's where he died! Stop, stop the car! But no one was allowed there. There was no marker, no sign. The Germans feared that neo-Nazis would turn the place into a shrine. I realized again that even though the Holocaust didn't affect my family directly, it had traumatized me anyway, feelings that I had long repressed. Because memories are often wrong, I recently searched the extensive material on Hitler's bunker. It turns out that my recollections are accurate. *The Fuhrerbunker* was located under the garden of the Reich Chancellery, which was leveled by Soviet forces in April 1945. At the time of my visit to Berlin, the site was indeed a weed-grown lot with a mound surrounded by a chain-link fence, on Wilhelmstrasse, near the Berlin Wall. After the reunification of Germany, the authorities built housing on the site, but it was not until June 2006 that they put up a large sign with photos, text, and a schematic drawing showing what the underground bunker looked like.

When I returned to New York, I told Lynn about Berlin and the feelings it stirred up. There were other signs of my Jewish awakening over the next months and years. While watching *Schindler's List*, Steven Spielberg's 1993 movie about the Holocaust and the "righteous gentile" who saved Jewish lives, I was moved not just by the black-and-white scenes of the concentration camps and Oscar Schindler's risky heroism, but by the Technicolor scene at the end when aging survivors, observing Jewish practice, placed small pebbles on the tombstones of those who didn't make it. They all looked like my parents, who were now dead, and I couldn't stop sobbing. Our daughter, Sarah, was turning 13 about then, and as her Bat Mitzvah approached, I started to reclaim my ability to read Hebrew, which had withered like an atrophied muscle. We began attending Friday evening services – not every week, but often.

And so, in my early 50s, married to an observant Jew, and raising my children as Jews, I was finally shaking my old feelings of the Jew as victim – passive victim – of the discrimination faced by my parents' generation and by the Nazi murder that hit us all. I could finally, emotionally, fully accept my Jewish identity, that I was a Shapiro as well as a Shepard. But it took a trip to the belly of the beast – Berlin, 40 years after the war – to start coming to terms with my childhood anxiety.

THREE

Jew vs. Jew: Philip Roth's *Eli, The Fanatic*

Just when I thought I had resolved my conflicted feelings about being Jewish, I am being tested anew by an astonishing religious revival now unfolding among Orthodox Jews in New York City and its suburbs. Although the percentage of Orthodox Jews is only about 10% nationally, it is exploding in the New York area. According to a report from the UJA-Federation of New York,[1] the Orthodox now account for 32% of the Jews in New York City, Long Island, and Westchester County – up from 13% in 1981.[2] More than two-thirds of them belong to Hasidic and other ultra-Orthodox sects. Because of high birth rates, two out of three school-age Jewish children in the New York region are Orthodox, most of them from ultra-Orthodox sects. In a couple of generations, if present trends continue, the ultra-Orthodox will represent a majority of all Jews in New York and its suburbs.

If your image of a Jewish New Yorker is an assimilated,

well-to-do, college-educated professional with liberal political views, think again. In general, ultra-Orthodox Jews are poorer, narrowly educated, and more politically conservative than Jews in general. Many of the ultra-Orthodox Jews are concentrated in Borough Park, Williamsburg, and other areas of Brooklyn, but they also live in many other neighborhoods, including the Upper West Side, usually thought of as the epicenter of liberal, assimilated Jewry.

When the state of Israel was established in 1948, it was widely assumed that the small number of Hasidic Jews were a remnant of pre-war Europe who, like some endangered species, would simply fade away in the new state of Israel. To help them cope with modern life, the Israeli government granted special privileges to this small group: they were exempt from military service; they controlled Sabbath laws, including a ban on public transportation; and they were given authority over certain family practices in Israel, including marriage and divorce. In the end, the ultra-Orthodox community grew in both number and political power, gaining the clout they wield today as a key part of the conservative coalition that governs Israel.

Like many Jews, I thought that America was different, that the desire to assimilate – to be American – would overwhelm those few remaining ultra-Orthodox Jews. And for many years, that felt true. When I was growing up in the Bronx, the handful of old-world Jews seemed willing to relinquish many of the traditional ways for the opportunity to blend in, the better to make it in America. Now, the strong and visible rise in the ultra-Orthodox population has caused a certain amount of unease among many Jews. Yes, that includes me.

In thinking about these feelings, I'm reminded of a short story that Philip Roth wrote in 1959, called *Eli, The Fanatic*, which was included in Roth's first book, a collection called *Goodbye, Columbus*. It has stayed in my memory for many years, largely because it struck a sensitive nerve: the issue of what kind of Jew I should be.

Eli, The Fanatic was published just 14 years after the end of World War II, and the story it tells is set in 1948, when memories of the Holocaust were still raw. Like many early Roth stories, it is set in the suburbs, some newly opened to the emerging Jewish middle class. But the story goes well beyond the satire of *Goodbye, Columbus*, the better-known title story in the collection.

The fictional town is called Woodenton, home to assimilated and eager-to-belong Jews. They are upset because an Orthodox Jew, a displaced person from Germany named Leo Tzuref, has opened a Talumudic school on a nearby hill to introduce 18 yarmulke-wearing boys, orphaned in the war, to the ritualistic life. The modern Jews of Woodenton are especially appalled when Tzuref dispatches a strange man to run errands in the town. He's the real thing, the assimilationists' nightmare: a bearded Holocaust survivor with sidelocks curled on his cheeks, clad in black coat and black wide-brimmed hat. He doesn't speak, the very symbol of the unspeakable. The townspeople call him "greenie," a callous shorthand for greenhorn.

"Goddam fanatics," says Ted, one of the Jews in town. "This is the 20th century.... Now it's the guy in the hat. Pretty soon all the little Yeshiva boys'll be spilling down into town."

Then, with Roth at his ironic best, Ted adds without a moment's thought: "Next thing they'll be after our daughters."

Another Jewish neighbor mocks Judaism itself: "This Abraham in the bible was going to kill his own kid for a sacrifice. You call that religion? ...Today a guy like that they'd lock him up..."

Ted and the other modern Jews of Woodenton enlist their neighbor, a lawyer named Eli Peck, to tell Tzuref that the zoning laws do not permit a boarding school of any kind in a residential area. The school is illegal and must close. After writing to Tzuref, Eli goes to visit him at the yeshiva. But Tzuref, in a funny bit of Talmudic dueling, outwits Eli. After more pressure from his Jewish neighbors, Eli writes Tzuref another letter, saying in part:

"...Woodenton, as you may not know, has long been the home of well-to-do Protestants. It is only since the war that Jews have been able to buy property here, and for Jews and Gentiles to live beside each other in amity. For this adjustment to be made, both Jews and Gentiles alike have had to give up some of their more extreme practices in order not to threaten or offend the other..."

Then, blaming the victim, Eli adds:

"...Perhaps if such conditions had existed in pre-war Europe, the persecution of the Jewish people, of which you and those 18 children have been victims, could not have been carried out with such success..."

Eli ultimately agrees that the Yeshiva can remain in its hilltop location, but he sets two conditions, including one requiring visitors coming to town to dress appropriately "in clothing usually associated with American life in the 20th century." Eli donates two suits to the greenie, along with shirts, shoes, underwear, a tie, and a new hat. The greenie sends him in return his own orthodox outfit, black hat and all.

Slowly, Eli undergoes a transformation, almost a religious conversion. Touched by the greenie's mute plight, he begins to empathize with the suffering of the survivors and feels a moral obligation to perpetuate the nearly obliterated civilization of his ancestors. He becomes convinced the refugees should be allowed to stay unconditionally in Woodenton.

He dons the greenie's black clothes. "For the first time in his life," Roth writes, "he *smelled* the color of blackness," his own long-repressed, deeply embedded identity. He parades around town, wearing the dress of the fanatics. "Horns blew, traffic jerked, as Eli made his way up Coach House Road... Shortly everybody in Coach House Road was aware that Eli Peck, the nervous young attorney with the pretty wife, was having a breakdown. Everyone except Eli Peck. He knew what he did was not insane, though he felt every inch of its strangeness. He felt those black clothes as if they were the skin of his skin..."

Eli marches to the hospital to see his newborn son, only to be dismissed as the victim of a nervous breakdown. The doctors inject him with a tranquilizer. "The drug calmed his soul," Roth writes in the story's last line, "but did not touch it down where the blackness had reached."

Roth's parable raises many issues, and one of them is very similar to a theme in Abraham Cahan's immigrant novel, *The Rise of David Levinsky*, written more than 40 years earlier: There is a price to be paid for rejecting one's heritage in the process of assimilation. It was true on Cahan's Lower East Side, and it was true in Roth's suburbia. For Eli, caught between tradition and modernity, between the Orthodox and the secular, the price was too high.

There are degrees of assimilation, of course, and not every Jew trying to make it in America is hostile to the older ways of being Jewish. By exaggerating the response in the fictionalized Woodenton, Roth is able to lay bare the conflicted feelings of Jews in transition from ghetto to suburb. The story, one of Roth's best, still resonates in me nearly 60 years after it was written.

Roth's story, it turns out, is based on a real episode that happened in 1948. A Holocaust survivor named Rabbi Michael Weissmandl established a Yeshiva in Westchester County, just north of New York City, for the orphaned children of a destroyed Yeshiva in Czechoslovakia.[3] Some members of the community objected, bringing the case to the local zoning board. But there was a crucial difference. In the real episode, it was chiefly gentiles who were complaining. By re-imagining the townspeople as Jews, Roth was able to explore the more complex feelings of Jews toward other Jews during a period of rapid assimilation in post-war America.

Coming of age years later, when the process of assimilation was far along, I took an unspoken pride in the accomplishments of Jews – their success in academia, business, media, politics, culture, and social causes. That pride could some-times be arrogant, leading to a form of Jewish exceptionalism. ("Did you know that Jews, who account for only 0.2% of the world's population, have won 22% of all Nobel Prizes?") But generally speaking, most of us quietly embraced this image of American Jewry: assimilated, accomplished, and morally con-cerned. Yes, we had something to prove: What better way to undermine the old stereotypes of Jews, to show we belong, to counter anti-Semitism?

Now things are changing again. Do I really want the new ultra-Orthodox to remind me and everyone else of the old world? Do I want them, soon to be the Jewish majority in New York, to be the face of American Jewry, to represent every-thing I don't want to be?

Though I recognize my own intolerance, I can easily see why the ultra-Orthodox get under my skin. They're an insular group, set in their ways, unreceptive to reason, and dismissive of less-observant Jews as not really Jewish. Who are they to define Judaism? Because Ultra-Orthodox men are very nar-rowly educated and usually don't work at jobs in the secular world, levels of poverty in the Ultra-Orthodox community are quite high: about one-fifth of Jews live in poverty in the New York area, according to the UJA-Federation report.

Moreover, the Orthodox are devoutly conservative on most political issues – the only Jewish denomination in New York to vote for Donald Trump over Hillary Clinton.[4] Similarly, Presi-dent Obama's second-term effort to rein in Iran's nuclear pro-gram also split American Jews. Liberal Jews generally support-ed Obama, while more politically conservative Jews, including the ultra-Orthodox, tended to oppose Obama's agreement with Iran.

But there's more to it than image and politics. Like the townspeople of Woodenton, I seem to be projecting my own long-dormant anxiety about being Jewish on to today's more numerous ultra-Orthodox, as if their anachronistic image threatens my own identity. Every bone in my assimilated body vibrates against their fundamentalism, their extremism, their old-world lifestyle, their rejection of mainstream Jewry. Like other secular Jews in New York, I am on my way to being a minority within a minority. And I don't like it.

These feelings are not without that most Jewish reaction: I feel guilty. And that guilt brings me back to *Eli, The Fanatic*.

Eli, after all, had a point. Several points. Isn't my reaction to the ultra-Orthodox a form of Jewish anti-Semitism, as it was in Woodenton? And where's my compassion? As heirs to our Ashkenazi ancestors, the ultra-Orthodox evoke our collective link to the 800-year history of Yiddish-speaking Jews in Europe – including my great-grandparents whose children emigrated to America from their *shtetls* in Poland. And because that history ended in horror, don't their Orthodox descendants deserve our empathy? How can I callously wish them all away?

By all logic, I should react the way Eli did: change my views and accept the ultra-Orthodox for what they are. But even as I grapple with these issues and acknowledge my own guilty feelings, I sense that my discomfort with the ultra-Orthodox is likely to grow stronger as their tribe increases. I'm not proud of these feelings. I have work to do.

FOUR

Gansevoort Street: The World of *Our* Fathers

It's a short street, as New York thoroughfares go, running just four blocks from the Hudson River to 13th Street, near Eighth Avenue. It retains many of the old features of its meat-packing past — especially the cobblestone street and the two-story buildings with their metal canopies over narrow sidewalks. But it is quite fashionable these days, with trendy shops where truck bays once stood, fancy restaurants where cheap diners once served pre-dawn breakfast, and artisanal cheese stores where once there was nothing at all. Near the Hudson, there's an entrance to the High Line, that newly famous railroad spur transformed into chic urban park. Beside it stands the new Whitney Museum, the latest architectural triumph of Renzo Piano.

This is Gansevoort Street today, gentrified but still recognizable.[1]

For roughly 30 years, from FDR's presidency in the 1930s

to LBJ's in the 1960s, my father, William Shepard, worked at 40 Gansevoort Street, in a small office above a refrigerated warehouse with truck bays out front. Shep, as he was called at work, commuted there by subway everyday from the Bronx. He was the treasurer and credit manager for a small company named Producers Distributing Agency, a wholesaler that bought chickens, turkeys, and ducks from poultry producers around the country and sold them to retailers in New York.

Shep was at his desk at PDA every morning at 6AM, when butchers and grocers started picking up the poultry products in the truck bays below his office. His job was to make sure their credit was good before he released the merchandise. During the rest of the day, usually smoking a pipe, he handled various accounting chores and ran the small office of some 15 people. A sweet and generous man, stocky with rimless glasses, he worked hard, rarely getting home before 6 PM, when we all ate supper together. It was never called dinner.

The meat business, then as now, was sharply divided between the purveyors of kosher and non-kosher food. PDA distributed non-kosher poultry, even though the founding family was Jewish. PDA's non-kosher niche gave my father all the excuse he needed to change his name from the obviously Jewish Shapiro to something he deemed more acceptable in the *goyish* part of the food chain.

Gansevoort Street remained the center of the meat-packing trade in New York for more than 50 years. In the 1960s, the city built the Hunts Point Terminal Market in the South Bronx, and the meat and poultry wholesalers gradually left for those more modern facilities. PDA closed in the early 1970s, and the building was later demolished. In its place at 40 Gansevoort is now a co-op apartment building atop a hip boutique, full of chic clothing for women and men – a far cry from the distant day when butchers in blood-stained aprons walked the street.

My father's time on Gansevoort Street was all I knew of his working life. He started there before I was born and retired in 1967, when I had already launched my own career as a journalist. I visited him there many times when I was a kid. He let me play with the adding machines, a pre-computer mechanical device with a big handle that summed numbers with remarkable speed. My father, normally a modest, self-effacing man, wowed me with his ability to do the math in his head just as fast as the machine. He also let me take stuff home from the office supply cabinet – an array of pencils, pads, erasers and paper clips that became the tools of a kid who liked to write. One summer when I was in high school, I actually had a job at 40 Gansevoort, doing various clerical tasks.

For all those years, Shep worked for a man we all called Bib, an acronym for Benjamin I. Brown, who owned the company. Their relationship was partly a friendship, partly a custodial partnership is which Shep was nominally in charge when Bib was away, and partly a sometimes-tense business arrangement of boss and underling. The Shep-Bib relationship produced an unexpected bonus: I soon became friends with Bib's son, Don, and the two of us have remained exceptionally close for years. We have spent many hours discussing our fathers.

Bib created the business with his father, Ben Lipshitz, a charismatic man who had a utopian vision. Born near Odessa in 1885, Lipshitz emigrated to the U.S. when he was 15, finding work as a farm hand near Philadelphia and taking the owner's last name of Brown. Later, he heard about Jews who had established agricultural colonies, part of a back-to-the-land movement that would take Jews from East Coast tenements to settle in the American West. Ben Brown decided to form his own settlement, this one near Gunnison, Utah.

It took years to organize, but he eventually enlisted 75 families to move west in 1911 to form an agricultural colony called Clarion.[2] Like the *kibbutzim* in Israel decades later, Clarion was an effort to find prosperity and dignity, far removed from the urban ghettos that had defined Jewish-American identity. "We Jews...must create a new healthy condition here in this country that should serve as a model for our people everywhere," he wrote many years later.

Clarion failed in 1916, done in by poor soil, lack of water, and disputes among the settlers, a Yiddish-accented mix of labor Zionists, socialists, and Orthodox Jews who knew next-to-nothing about agriculture. Though most of the colonists returned to the East, Brown stayed on in Gunnison, forming the Utah Poultry Association to represent the poultry growers in the area. Through various mergers with growers in other states, Utah Poultry eventually became Norbest, the nation's oldest turkey marketing cooperative. Ben Brown, utopian Jewish pioneer, was now a big player in the non-kosher turkey business.

The impulse behind Clarion lived on. In 1934, Ben Brown and his second wife established a new Jewish commune in New Jersey, called Jersey Homesteads, which included a 1,100-acre farm, a housing development, and a factory that manufactured women's clothing. The town grew to more than 1,000 people, many of them Jewish garment workers, usually committed socialists, who had resettled from New York City. Ben Brown died of cancer in 1939, at age 54. The town he started was renamed Roosevelt, N.J. after the war and exists to this day.[3]

Meanwhile, Bib Brown, Ben's oldest child, was pursuing his own life. In 1929, he graduated from UCLA, earning a Phi Beta Kappa key and winning a fellowship to begin PhD studies in economics at the University of Wisconsin. It was not to be. Ben asked Bib to move to New York instead, to help set up a sales office for Norbest. That sales office ultimately became Producers Distributing Agency on Gansevoort Street.[4]

Bib, inheriting many of his father's political views, liked the idea of working with poultry growers organized into farmer-owned cooperatives. "I felt a great sympathy for the farmers who were having such a hard time making a living,"[5] he said in an interview with his stepdaughter many years later. Bib also was a supporter of trade unions, an unusual position for a businessman in the 1930s, and he had cordial labor relations with the unions that had organized the warehouse and office workers at PDA, as well as the company's truck drivers. But when he decided that PDA should get rid of its trucks and rely instead on contract haulers, the truckers union went on strike to protect their jobs. "After being in business for 40 years on a friendly basis with the unions, I was very upset when they called a strike on us," he later recalled. "It really was an unhappy time."[6]

As the strike by the truckers indicated, there was a deep

contradiction between Bib the business owner and Bib the left-wing economic thinker. My father had told me a bit about Bib's political views in the 1930s and 1940s, and there were even dark whispers that he was a Communist. I later learned that both Bib and his wife, Esther, were, in fact, members of the Communist Party for several years, leaving in 1939, along with many other American Jews, when Stalin and Hitler signed their non-aggression pact.[7] Don Brown recalls that his parents were afraid of being exposed as former Communists and were "scared stiff" that they would be forced to testify before the House Un-American Activities Committee in the late 1940s or early 1950s.[8] Even as late as the 1960s, when Bib ran for the local school board, he feared his Communist past would come back to haunt him.

During World War II, Bib volunteered for a commission in the U.S. Navy and was stationed in the Pacific. He wrote occasionally to my father, who was nominally in charge of the PDA office on Gansevoort Street. One such war-time letter from Bib, the only one that has survived, is dated January 24, 1944 and is addressed, "Dear Sheppy." Having heard that my father had been sick (a rare occurrence), Bib expressed his concern. He asked my father to send flowers to his wife, Esther, for Valentine's Day – "a large nice bouquet, including red roses" with a card saying: "To my beloved wife and our two little Valentines. (by order of) Lt. Bib." In closing, Bib said, "the news from Europe is wonderful these days and from here it will also be good – soon."

One of my earliest recollections of my father at work stems from an incident that occurred during World War II while Bib was in the Navy serving in the Pacific. It was recounted more than once over the years, becoming part of family lore:

> Many products were rationed during the war, including food, and the retailers served by PDA were entitled to only so much poultry or so many dozen eggs. But a flourishing black market existed, in which some large stores or chains would bribe food distributors to give them extra supplies. One day, a man came into my father's office and slipped him an envelope filled with hundreds of dollars, with the clear implication there was more to be had if he cooperated in the black market. Shep turned it down, later saying it was just plain wrong to take the money. He once told my sister and me that it wasn't right to capitalize on the situation when "our boys were fighting overseas." Yes, those were his words.

After Bib returned, the business flourished amid the post-war economic boom. Soon, though, contradictions arose between Bib the Business Man and Bib the Closeted Communist. When sales slowed, Bib was under pressure to cut costs and negotiate better deals – hence the fight with the truckers union. My parents saw him as rather tough-minded, or at least ungenerous, and certainly not grateful for Shep's manifold contributions to the company. In Shep's eyes, PDA was not exactly a workers' paradise.

Things came to a head during the early 1950s, when the business suffered from a failed expansion into frozen food, and Bib was forced to take out a mortgage on his house. After months of tension and fears of bankruptcy, Lever Brothers stepped in to buy the frozen food business from PDA, and PDA slowly regained its financial health.[9]

As the treasurer of PDA, my father understood full well the problems. At the same time, he was dealing with his own financial worries and his own insecurities. Shep thought he had been underpaid for years, but he never complained to Bib. Once, when he received what he thought was a paltry raise, my mother shouted to him: "Tell Bib to shove it up his kiester."

He didn't say anything of the sort to Bib, of course, and he didn't look for another job. Instead, he fretted about his lack of a college education and his failure to become a Certified Public Accountant. And when Bib offered him a chance to become a salesman, a more lucrative job, he turned it down. Shep, who didn't like asking anyone for anything, could no more be a salesman than an elephant could fly.

Towards the end of his working life, Shep worried about getting a pension from PDA, beyond what he was entitled to from Social Security. He felt he deserved a pension – in part, because he gave up his union membership (which provided a small pension) when he became part of PDA's management, and in part because he was a trustworthy steward of the business when Bib was in the Navy. As his retirement drew near in 1967, when he turned 70, Shep grew increasingly agitated. Afraid to ask, he wanted Bib to step up and bestow a pension on him as a kind of honorarium for his years of loyal service. Yes, the money was vital, but a pat on the back from Bib – his approval – seemed just as important.

In the end, my father, encouraged by my mother and me, finally broached the subject with Bib. I don't know whether Bib was willing or reluctant, but in any case he granted Shep a pension of $175 a month. As small as it sounds today, the pension more than covered the rent for my parents' rent-controlled apartment in the Bronx. (The pension was the equivalent in today's money of $1,284 a month.) Combined with social security and his own savings, he could afford to retire. The only hitch: the pension would last only 10 years. Like a container of milk, it had an expiration date.

Inevitably, the whole scenario played out again 10 years later. Again, my father became agitated, again he wanted Bib to take the initiative, and again he finally reached out to Bib. This time, Bib agreed to an extension, as well as a $25-a-month increase to partly compensate for inflation (the equivalent of another $183 a month in today's money). And this time there was no expiration date. Shep, then 80, finally had the security of a modest pension for life, as well as the goodwill he so desperately wanted from Bib.

My father died in 1983, at age 86, several years after Bib had retired to Florida.

I saw Bib from time to time when he visited Don in New York, and the conversation was poignant when his thoughts turned to the PDA years and to Shep. We even exchanged letters during the years I was editor of *Business Week*, focusing on the economic and political issues that so interested him. He died in 2008, just shy of his 100th birthday.

The Bib-Shep relationship has left an enduring legacy: Don Brown is one of my closest friends. It's not that I see him more than other friends. Not that we belong to the same profession.

Not, even, that we have a lot of the same interests. Rather, with our shared past, we have bonded with uncommon intimacy, like two Army buddies who had served together.

Donny, as I called him then, grew up in Mount Vernon, a largely Jewish outpost in Westchester County just north of the city. His parents weren't at all observant – Don had a confirmation, not a Bar Mitzvah – but they were early supporters of Israel, whose kibbutzim echoed the communal ethic of the Clarion colony in Utah.

I lived in the Bronx, so we didn't see each other much as kids. But in our college years, we stayed in touch and a friendship blossomed. When he was a doctor in the Peace Corps in El Salvador, I went to visit. When I was a correspondent in London, he came to stay with me. When my father died, he rode in the car with Lynn and me to the cemetery. It was always a personal friendship. We knew about each other's career ambitions, about our girlfriends, about our anxieties. And we knew about our fathers – their feelings, their frustrations, their relationship.

And yet, in the beginning at least, I felt something of the same upstairs-downstairs tension in our friendship that echoed my father's relationship with Bib. Once, when I was finishing high school at Bronx Science in the spring of 1956, my family visited the Browns in Mount Vernon. Donny's mother, Esther, asked me what college I had chosen for the fall. City College of New York, I replied. She noted that CCNY was famous for its basketball teams – a reference, I knew, to the great Cinderella team that had won both the NCAA and the NIT tournaments in 1950, only to be famously disgraced by a point-fixing scandal a year later. Esther's comment was true enough, but it felt to me as something of a put down. I welled up with defensiveness. Basketball? Doesn't she know about CCNY's academic reputation as the Proletarian Harvard? Doesn't she know that it had produced all those Nobel Laureates, public intellectuals, and famous writers? Or that it was tuition-free, as if we had all won scholarships?

I didn't say anything. But even at age 16 I understood what was going on. Bib was my father's boss, and Donny was the boss's son. They lived where the rich people lived, Donny drove a red convertible to A.B. Davis High School, and his sister went to Radcliffe. I was Shep's son, and we lived in the Bronx – not poverty-stricken, but not able to afford a house in Westchester County, to say nothing of any red convertible or fancy college.

Envious? Yes, of course.

I consoled myself by knowing that I was going to college a year ahead of Donny, even though we were exactly the same age. I had skipped the eighth grade thanks to a program in the city called Special Progress, SP for short, which enabled smart kids to go right from the seventh grade to the ninth. I was quietly thrilled to realize they didn't have the SPs in the suburbs. They didn't have the Bronx High School of Science, either. I felt a little better.

In retrospect, it seems clear I was fighting my father's battle. As a kid, I bought into his version of events: He was the devoted employee who worked 11 hours a day starting at 6 AM. He was underappreciated and underpaid. He had to beg for a pension. He wasn't recognized for his loyal stewardship of PDA during the war. And the villain of the piece was Bib, that hypocrite who professed to be concerned about the working class but really cared only about his business. I would make things right: I would be the success Shep wasn't. I would show them just how good I was.

With a chip on my shoulder the size of a two-by-four, every rung up the professional ladder was payback. Teaching at Columbia. *So there!* Senior Editor at *Newsweek*. Take that! Editor-In-Chief of *Business Week*. *Not bad for a Bronx boy!* Elected to the Magazine Editors Hall of Fame. *Did you hear that?* Dean of a journalism school. *Enough said!*

And yet, as I got older, I began to have some doubts about the received narrative of the Bib-Shep relationship. Whether Bib was fair or not, my father surely bore some of the blame for his own predicament. Why didn't he stick up for himself? Ask for a bigger raise? Why didn't he seize the opportunity to be a salesman? Or look for another job? Even my mother said my father was too nice for his own good. What she really meant, I realized, was that he was too passive.

I became racked with guilt over the prospect of doing better than my father, ashamed of the very ambition. Failure was not an option, but success carried with it the guilt that came with outdoing my father and pleasing my mother. Ambition was best kept hidden. Was it any wonder that I chose to wear the disguise of an engineering student rather than declare my real interest in literature, my goal of becoming a journalist?

At first, I rarely talked about any of this to anyone, certainly not Don, and I hid both my anger and ambition, concealed by an easy-going manner. But as we started to become good friends, I broached the subject and was stunned to realize that he, too, wanted to talk about our fathers. Don, for all his advantaged background, had his own set of problems. One of them, to my amazement, was money. Not that he didn't have enough, but rather he had trouble spending it. On a trip we took together to Spain in the late 1960s, Don spent a lot of valuable tourist time hunting for the cheapest gas station. He quibbled over restaurant bills. It was clear that he rarely felt comfortable parting with a buck. I, by contrast, had no problem spending the money I had, treating myself to things I wanted.

As I learned more, I realized that Don's problems were the mirror image of mine: Guilt about his privileged upbringing – symbolized by that red convertible – and hurt by issues with his own father, who turned out to be hard to please. Don's career path reflected his concerns. He was determined to do good in the world. He went to medical school, served as a doctor in the Peace Corps, and focused his career on "community psychiatry." Though he maintained a small private practice, he mostly developed and led clinical programs for immigrants and indigents, as well as treating patients with long-term mental illness. In an unintended irony, many of his patients lived in the Bronx, not far from my old neighborhood.

Over the years, all of this became grist for our conversational mill. For a time, we went to dinner with our wives, and as enjoyable as those evenings were, we gradually turned them into regular boys' nights out. There was just too much personal stuff to talk about. Helped greatly by years of psychoanalysis, both Don and I gradually overcame most of our personal demons. I like to think our conversations played a role, too.

Our friendship has lasted some 60 years now. It is deep, personal, and full of affection. And it stands as a proud heritage of the time Bib and Shep worked together on Gansevoort Street, in those long-ago days when it was truly a meat-packing district.

FIVE

Is Willy Loman Jewish?
Does it Matter?

I first read *Death of A Salesman* when I was in college, about a decade after it opened on Broadway in 1949, and I was immediately drawn to it. Arthur Miller's masterpiece made an American Everyman out of its protagonist, Willy Loman, whose plight resonated with audiences everywhere. And to me nothing was more resonant than the emotionally wrenching father-son relationship between Willy and his boys, especially Biff, the eldest. At times, it struck home.

Right off the bat, let me say that Shep was no Willy. He didn't have Willy's false values, his delusions of grandeur, or the marital infidelity that undermined Willy in the eyes of his son. But I must admit I've had moments of filial discomfort every time I've watched or read the play. Like Willy, Shep did not achieve financial success, a major issue in both households. Like Willy, Shep felt underappreciated by his boss, reduced to pleading for money. And, every so often, it even felt to me that Willy was Jewish, which only deepened the similarities between Shep and Willy – while increasing my own anxiety. Miller went to great lengths to deny that Willy was Jewish. To drive home the Everyman theme, he stripped the Loman family of any religion or ethnicity, any heritage or tradition. They were quite unlike O'Neill characters who were undeniably Irish Catholic or an Odets family that was explicitly Jewish. In the words of one critic, Willy was "ethnically anonymous." [1]

Yet, almost from the beginning, some critics thought that Willy was Jewish, like his creator, and that the Loman family saga was a second-generation immigrant story, not unlike my own. Such speculation was supported by the play's dialogue, some of which has the cadence of Yiddish, most famously in the play's most memorable line: "Attention, attention must finally be paid to such a person."

It didn't take long for someone to stage a Yiddish version. In June 1949, just four months after the Broadway opening, a Yiddish translation called *Toyt fun a Salesman*, appeared in Argentina. Produced by the husband-wife team of Joseph Buloff and Luba Kadison, it moved in 1951 to Brooklyn, Willy Loman's backyard. Miller saw the Brooklyn performance and became friends with Buloff and Kadison.[2] Theater critic George Ross, writing in *Commentary* magazine in 1951 about the Brooklyn production, put it bluntly: "What one feels most strikingly is that this Yiddish play is really the original, and the Broadway production was merely Arthur Miller's translation into English." [3]

Out of curiosity, I went to see a Yiddish production staged

in New York in the fall of 2015 by the New Yiddish Rep[4], a theater company that has also produced a Yiddish version of *Waiting for Godot*. Their productions employ supertitles in English, projected on a wall, for the benefit of people like me who don't speak Yiddish. I was accompanied by a friend, Darlene Ehrenberg, whose first language was Yiddish and who is still fluent. Like others in the audience, she felt that this Yiddish version was more powerful than Miller's original. I could only regret that I never learned the Yiddish that my mother spoke to my grandmother when I was a boy.

Was the Loman family Jewish? Critic Leslie Fiedler said yes.[5] So did playwright David Mamet, whose grandfather was a travelling salesman, "an everyday figure of American Jewish life in the first and second generation," he wrote. "Willy Loman...is, to any Jew, unmistakably a Jew." [6] Playwright Tony Kushner, also Jewish, tends to dance around the question. It's hard to tell, he said at a New York forum celebrating the centennial of Miller's birth, because the language is "very New York, very urban." While stressing the political themes in the play, especially Miller's critique of capitalism, Kushner did concede that "I sort of feel like it's a Jewish thing. There is a *Yiddishkeit* thing going on." [7]

Miller spent years denying that Willy was Jewish, in large part because he didn't want the play to be defined by any specific ethnicity that he feared might render it parochial. In 1969, 20 years after opening night, Miller declared in an interview that Willy's religious or cultural background "seems to me irrelevant." [8] He stripped Willy of anything that smacked of Jewishness. Willy's father was a mythic pioneer in the American

West, while his brother Ben made a fortune in an undefined jungle somewhere far away. And, as critic Julius Novick put it, "Who ever heard of nice Jewish boys named Biff and Happy." [9] Was it really necessary to portray Willy without any religion or ethnicity in order to endow him with universal meaning? After all, many other ethnic protagonists in theater and literature achieved universal greatness, including, most obviously, the Irish Catholics in Eugene O'Neill, but also the genteel Southerners in Tennessee Williams, and the blacks from Pittsburgh's Hill District in August Wilson.

Some critics think Willy would have been a richer, more authentic character if he were distinctly Jewish. Leslie Fiedler accused Miller of pursuing a "pseudo universality" by creating "crypto Jews." [10] To Fiedler, Willy was thus less authentic. Mary McCarthy agreed: Willy is "a capitalized Human Being without being anyone...Willy is only a type." [11] Julius Novick also thinks the Lomans' ethnicity matters, but for an entirely different reason: "Their separation from their roots, their isolation..." this is what makes them terribly vulnerable to the false values that undo them." In fact, Novick thinks Miller knew exactly what he was doing: the lack of ethnicity, he writes, "was an integral part of their characterization." [12]

Despite Miller's effort to deracinate the Loman family, there is plenty of evidence of Willy's Jewish provenance. When he was a teenager, Miller wrote two unpublished short stories about Jewish salesmen. According to Miller scholar Christopher Bigsby[13], one of the stories, *In Memorium*, is a clear precursor to *Salesman*. It's about a Jewish salesman named Alfred Schoenzeit who is crushed by the Depression and, according to Miller's notes, commits suicide by jumping in front of an oncoming New York subway train. In *Timebends*, his 1987 autobiography, Miller provides another hint when he says he based Willy, in part, on his uncle, Manny Newman, a travelling salesman from Brooklyn who preferred fantasy to truth.[14]

Finally, in 1999, on the 50th anniversary of the play's debut, Miller reluctantly conceded that the Loman family was Jewish. But he insisted that they were assimilated beyond the point of any Jewish identity. The Lomans, he said, were "Jews light years away from religion or community." Then, stressing again his political point of view, he wrote, "they exist in a spot that most Americans feel they inhabit – on the sidewalk side of the glass looking in on a well-lighted place." [15]

Why such a long-delay in acknowledging Willy's Jewish roots? At the time Miller wrote *Salesman*, he was clearly trying to transcend his own Jewishness. In *Timebends*, he wrote of his desire to "identify myself with mankind rather than one small tribal fraction of it." [16] Sound familiar? My own early ambivalence about being Jewish was not so far removed from Miller's – adding to my fascination with *Salesman*.

There are many other examples of Miller's conflicted feelings about his Jewishness. On the one hand, he wrote affectionately in *Timebends* of sitting on his great-grandfather's lap in a synagogue, and he painted a warm picture of Jewish Harlem in the 1920s.[17] He attacked anti-Semitism in his 1945 novel, *Focus*. And he wrote two plays about the Holocaust, *Incident at Vichy*, first produced in 1964, and *Broken Glass* in 1994.

Yet, he also wrote in *Timebends* about his embarrassment as a schoolboy when he didn't want to tell a librarian that his father's name was Isidore, which he knew sounded very Jewish. [18] And at the time of his first marriage, to a lapsed Catholic named Mary Grace Slattery, he declared that "Judaism for me and Catholicism for Mary were dead history...devised primarily to empower the priesthood by setting people against one another." [19] Miller went on to two more marriages, both to non-Jews, including Marilyn Monroe, the ultimate *shiksa* goddess.

Whatever his reasons for denying Willy his Jewishness, it is hard to argue that Miller lost much by eliminating Willy's roots. We certainly get the picture of a family in Brooklyn struggling to make ends meet, riven by father-son strife and marital infidelity, while barely held together by a much put-upon wife. Does it matter whether they are Jewish, Irish, Italian, or nothing? The play works on its own terms, after all, and Willy does achieve universal appeal. Why else was it so successful for so many years in so many venues, including China? Yet Willy's Jewishness does matter to me in a very personal way: it adds to the father-son angst I feel whenever I think about the play.

I sense other parallels as well. It turns out that Miller had his own issues with his father. He clearly wanted the play to be seen as a critique of capitalism – in large part because of his own family's searing experience during the Depression. His father, Isidore, was illiterate, but nonetheless ran a successful coat-manufacturing business so prosperous that he rode to work in the Garment District in a chauffeur-driven limousine. [20] But his business failed, after he made some imprudent investments in the stock market, when Arthur was only 14. [21] Isidore was forced to move the family from its large Manhattan apartment, with a view of Central Park, to a small house in Brooklyn, "a chicken coop of a house," Miller later wrote.[22] While still in high school, Miller became a Socialist. "Marxism... was a way of forgiving my father," he wrote in *Timebends*, "for it showed him as a kind of digit in a nearly cosmic catastrophe that was beyond his powers to avoid."[23] Like me, Miller was fighting his father's battle. While I focused on the microcosm of Shep's working life on Gansevoort Street, Miller chose the larger playing field of politics as his battleground.

Miller's radicalism remained deep his entire life, and he frequently referred to its 1930s roots. "The Depression was only incidentally a matter of money," he wrote more than 50 years later. "Rather it was a moral catastrophe, a violent revelation of the hypocrisies behind the façade of American society."[24]

Miller's anti-capitalist views were reflected in parts of *Salesman*. In a famous scene near the end, Willy confronts his boss, who is about to fire him after a lifetime of work: "All I need is $40 a week. You can't eat the orange and throw the peel away...a man is not a piece of fruit!" The details are very different, but I confess to thinking of the old Shep-Bib tension, when my father, about to retire, had to plead with his boss for a pension.

Like Gatsby in an entirely different milieu, Willy was intended as a symbol of the American Dream gone awry. But when the play opened in 1949, America was enjoying a post-war boom, fresh from its victory over Axis evil, and full of optimism. That was hardly fertile ground for a play critical of America's economic system — and few critics saw it that way. Rather, it was widely viewed as the tragedy of a man done in by his own delusions and false values — more personal than political.

Brian Dennehy, who played Willy in the 1999 Broadway revival and a subsequent TV production, agrees that the play retains its great popularity because audiences identify with the family themes in the play, not its politics. That's why, he said at a recent forum, it carries an emotional wallop that leaves audiences in tears.[25]

Having been moved to tears every time I see the play, I know I'm not crying because of the shortcomings of capitalism. It's the personal tragedy of Willy that gets me – the self-deluding man who embraces all the wrong values, teaches his sons all the wrong lessons, and eventually destroys his family and himself. The political message is secondary at best.

Miller never gave up his view that his plays should be polemical. As he wrote nearly 40 years later in his autobiography, "I still thought writing had to try to save America, and that meant grabbing people and shaking them by the back of the neck."[26] Was he in denial about any interpretation of *Salesman* other than political? Why didn't he fully acknowledge Willy's complicity in his own downfall? Or that father-son tension is a very familiar dynamic that could occur in any economic system?

I can only conclude that Arthur Miller wasn't his own best critic, his own best interpreter. Perhaps it doesn't matter. Surely it's enough that in Willy Loman he created a character that continues to move people deeply, a travelling salesman who has special meaning for me. Yes, attention must be paid to such a person.

SIX

My Encounter
With Isaac Bashevis Singer

Musing about my past had an unintended consequence: It reinforced my interest in the vast literature of Jewish immigration. I had read some of it – by such writers as Abraham Cahan, Anzia Yezerska, and Henry Roth – but very little by the most famous immigrant writer of them all: Isaac Bashevis Singer, who wrote in Yiddish and won the Nobel Prize for Literature in 1978. So I signed up to audit a class on Singer in the Jewish Studies Department at the City College of New York, from which I had graduated a lifetime ago.

There I was, on a bright, sunny day in September 2014, riding the Number 1 subway to 137th Street, the City College station just two stops north of Columbia University, but a world apart. I trudged up the steep hill from Broadway to Amsterdam Avenue, catching sight of the neo-Gothic buildings, vintage 1907, now gloriously restored. Beyond my interest in Singer and his brilliant stories, I was curious to see what it was like now that the student body at CCNY was dramatically changed from the "Proletarian Harvard" era of my day. I entered the North Academic Center, a sprawling, ugly building that didn't exist back then, and found my way to Room 4-209. There were ten students besides me: six women and four men. The class was smaller than I imagined, more a seminar than a lecture. But the real shocker was that I was the only white student in the room. Perhaps I shouldn't have been surprised: About 70% of the undergraduates at City College these days are students of color, many of them immigrants – and the school is one of the most diverse in the country, with undergraduates who speak more than 90 languages. But this was the Jewish Studies Department, after all, and I just assumed most of the students would be Jewish.

I couldn't have been more wrong. I soon learned that the department has about 70 students majoring in Jewish studies and 120 or so minoring in it – and 95% of them are not Jewish. As far as I can tell, it is the only Jewish studies department at any major American college in which the majority of the students are not Jewish. Nearly ten years earlier, Samuel Freedman wrote a story about the City College program in the *New York Times* – marveling at the same student profile that so amazed me.[1] I couldn't help but wonder why so many non-Jewish students were registered for a course in the Jewish Studies Department about a Yiddish writer who died in 1991.

The department was established in 1970 and generously funded in 2008 by Michael Ross, a City College alum who made it big as a Hollywood writer and producer. Over the years it was built into a prestigious program by Professor Roy

Mittelman, a former rabbi, who established a rigorous curriculum offering courses in Jewish history, religion, and literature. A small department in a large college, it had developed a reputation as a welcoming place that looked after its students with plenty of academic support and extracurricular counseling. The Singer course was taught by Dr. Amy Kratka, a young, tenured faculty member, whose friendly manner personified the department. On the first day, she asked the students to introduce themselves and to say something unusual about their backgrounds or interests. To show everyone what she had in mind, she started the process. She was a CUNY product herself, she said, earning her BA degree at Queens College, then getting her PhD at Boston University, where she wrote her dissertation on Cynthia Ozick. She was married to a criminal lawyer and had three children: two girls, seven and ten, and a boy not quite three who, she told us, was about to get his first haircut. She spoke Hebrew and some Yiddish and had taught in the department for several years.

One by one, the students spoke, some in accented English, most of them shy, as if they were afraid of saying the wrong thing. I was eager to hear why they were taking the Singer course. One young man, an English major, registered because it looked like an interesting literature class. A woman applying to medical school signed up to relieve her heavy load of lab courses. Another man, an immigrant from Bangladesh majoring in psychology, was interested in the immigrant experience described by Singer, hoping to find parallels with his own background. Besides, he said, he was a Muslim wanting to learn a little more about Jewish culture. Nearly all of them later told me that they were attracted to the course because Amy Kratka was such a good teacher. Some knew of her from a previous course, others from word of mouth and those ubiquitous student ratings available online.

When it was my turn to speak, I told them briefly about my career as a magazine editor, my role as founding dean at the CUNY Graduate School of Journalism, and my interest in Jewish writers. I went on to say that when I was an undergraduate at City College, the North Academic Center didn't exist. On this very site was Lewisohn Stadium (demolished in 1973), where I, as a member of the CCNY freshmen baseball team, came to practice most spring days. Judging from the astonished expressions around me, I might as well have said I was from ancient Mesopotamia. But I managed to bond a bit with most of the students during small breakout groups and pre-class chatter throughout the semester.

The course itself was a delight, rigorous but enjoyable. Amy Kratka was as advertised: deeply knowledgeable, but a down-to-earth teacher skilled at drawing out students who didn't know much about Judaism. They usually had worthwhile things to say, often tapping their own disparate experiences to provide refreshing insights.

The course tried to understand Singer's literature in the context of his own unusual life: growing up the son of a rabbi in Poland; struggling to become a writer in the shadow of his older brother; emigrating to the U.S. in 1935; suffering the loneliness of assimilation; and overcoming the challenge of writing in Yiddish, an 800-year-old language that all but died during the Holocaust. And, of course, his eventual emergence

as one of the great story-tellers of the 20th century, a writer who vividly captured the universal meaning of a forgotten
world for American readers. When he won the Nobel Prize in
Literature in 1978, he delivered the first line of his acceptance
speech in Yiddish.

Besides dozens of short stories and two novels, we read
two biographies. One was a probing literary history by Janet Hadda, a Yiddish-speaking scholar and psychoanalyst at
UCLA, who scrutinized his work by linking it to his own
traumas.[2] The other was a memoir by Dvorah Telushkin, who
served as Singer's assistant in New York and provided a much
more anecdotal take on Singer's day-to-day life.[3] Especially in
his older years, Singer liked to come across as a grandfatherly
sort who fed the pigeons on Broadway and welcomed visitors,
but the books portray him as a self-absorbed, selfish man who
wasn't very nice to the people closest to him, including Alma,
his wife of 50 years, and an estranged son from an earlier relationship in Poland.

But what a storyteller. For Singer, the story was everything,
and he would probably have been appalled to see what has
happened to the study of literature in academia these days – all
that critical theory and textual deconstruction. In unadorned
prose, he spun yarns of simple people, whose folklore and mys-
ticism transcended time and place to probe universal themes.
We started with his stories for children, "the "best readers of
genuine literature," Singer called them. Then we moved on
over several weeks to perhaps 30 stories, including his most famous: *The Spinoza of Market Street*, *Short Friday*, and, of course,
Gimpel The Fool, translated into English by Saul Bellow in 1953.

It was that translation, released in the same year as Bellow's ground-breaking novel, *The Adventures of Augie March*, that brought Singer to the attention of American readers.

At times, Amy lectured. Or she asked questions, waiting patiently for the students to speak up. On some days, we broke into small discussion groups. Each student made an oral presentation and wrote two papers. Once, Amy showed the film of *Yentl, the Yeshiva Boy*, starring Barbara Streisand. Singer had been very upset with the film on the understandable ground that it corrupted his story. Yet it portrayed something of *shtetl* life in Eastern Europe and brought home the dilemma of ambitious girls in a patriarchal society.

The first novel on our reading list was Singer's first book, *Satan in Goray*, published in 1935, just before Singer came to America. I wasn't looking forward to reading it. Did I really care about a story set in 17th century Poland, about the coming of a false messiah to the fictional town of Goray? Especially when the novel was full of mystical happenings that defied immediate understanding?

Yet I was mesmerized, swept along by Singer's ability to tell a powerful tale. I felt, as the town people felt, the fantastic allure of a messiah who would relieve all their burdens. I even understood, with some extra reading, the religious fervor of a mad young woman, Rechele, possessed by a dybbuk. And how, according to Hadda's biography, Rechele was based on Singer's sister, who was an epileptic, commonly thought in the folklore of the time, to be a person possessed by demons. Judging by their comments, the students were also taken with the story.

The second novel we read, *Enemies, A Love Story*, was one of the few Singer stories set in America. The protagonist is Herman Broder, who survived the Holocaust by hiding for three years in a hayloft in Poland, protected and cared for by a young peasant woman named Yadwiga. After the war, told that his wife, Tamara, and their two children had been killed by the Nazis, he marries Yadwiga and emigrates to New York. Herman soon after has an affair with Masha, another Holocaust survivor, who wants to marry him. A bit later, Tamara, the wife he thought dead, turns up in New York (her children had been killed) and makes her claim on Herman. There he is, one man with three women. At the end, Masha commits suicide, and Yadwiga gives birth to Herman's child. Herman disappears and Tamara ends up caring for Yadwiga and her new child. The novel was made into a wonderful movie in 1989, written and directed by Paul Mazursky, starring Ron Silver as Herman Broder.

I felt great empathy for Herman, a man who just could not move on, could not overcome the trauma of the Holocaust. He disappears, retreating from reality by, in effect, finding a new hayloft, this one in America. Much to my surprise, the students, particularly the women, had little sympathy for him. They saw him as a selfish man who would not take responsibility for himself. "He was an asshole," one young woman said in a small discussion group. The men seemed more divided. Was it a gender issue? Or an ethnic issue? Was I, a Jewish man, more sympathetic to a Holocaust survivor, no matter how self-absorbed and irresponsible? I found myself wondering whether these women of color were particularly angry at men who shirked responsibility? Or was I being a racist for thinking so?

And so it went: the students were able to think about the stories in the context of their own immigrant experiences. Their reactions enriched my own understanding of the Yiddish culture of pre-war Europe, of the Jewish immigrant experience in America, and of the broader struggle other groups had in the process of assimilation. For the first time, I understood Singer's universal appeal when I saw how ten diverse students, none of them Jewish, engaged so enthusiastically in the literature from another time and place.

Beyond that, I experienced an unusual and personal homecoming. Sitting as a student once again at City College, I realized that for all the upheaval that had convulsed the campus since I had graduated, the school's working-class mission was much the same as 50 years ago, or even 100 years ago when the students were mostly immigrant Jews. City College had survived the race riots of 1969, the cauldron of open admissions, and the vast demographic change in its student body. It was now more than a decade into a strong turnaround driven by higher standards. Though it is no longer tuition-free and graduation rates are lower than in my day, City College's core values are intact. It knows what it stands for.

I was sad when the course ended. However enjoyable and enlightening it had been, however reminiscent of my time as a student, I felt the years pressing in. I had recently retired from a lifetime of work – an old man, I'm sure, in the eyes of the students. Their lives, however uncertain, lay before them. I was looking back, the past beckoning me to a kind of summing up, as if I could tabulate my life's pluses and minuses on the adding machine in my father's office on Gansevoort Street.

Yes, I had come a long way from my City College days, more successful than I had dared to dream, but I was feeling more nostalgic than joyful, searching my dimming memory for any shards that would bring greater clarity and meaning.

I walked slowly to the subway after the last class. Rain had started to fall, but somehow it didn't seem right to hail a cab.

SEVEN

The Immigrants From Kolomaya

And what about my own immigrant roots? Reading Isaac Bashevis Singer triggered thoughts about my mother's passage to America and about the Tanner side of my family. I knew little of it, and had never much cared about it. Like my mother, I thought it a world best left behind. The only grandparent I knew was my mother's mother, Millie, who was my only direct connection to the old country they all wanted to forget – as if by not talking about it, they could make it disappear, like an early morning fog. But Grandma Millie died when I was ten, and my mother claimed ignorance of her roots.

I did know that my mother, born in London, came to New York as a young girl. And I knew, despite her reluctance to acknowledge it, that her family originally hailed from some place in Eastern Europe – and that her Tanner maiden name was originally Tanenzapf. That was it, the sum total of my knowledge of the old world and of my maternal-side heritage.

My only other link to the distant past was through my mother's much-revered older brother, Lou Tanner. Unlike my parents, Uncle Lou was well educated, a star student. A graduate of the much-acclaimed Townsend Harris High School,[1] then a special three-year program for smart boys, Uncle Lou went on to City College, then earned a master's degree in chemistry from MIT in 1924. Pretty impressive stuff for an immigrant Jew whose first language was Yiddish – and a not-so-subtle lesson for me.

There were many stories about Uncle Lou circulating in our household. One, that he himself told, concerned a visit to the United States by Albert Einstein in 1921. One of his lectures was at City College, and afterward Uncle Lou remembers Einstein getting into a car. My uncle then ran alongside the car as it slowly made its way through the gothic arches on Convent Avenue, jumping on the running board to get a close-up look at his hero. As a boy, I was wowed every time I heard the story.

Years later, I confirmed the basic facts of the story: On his very first visit to the United States in April 1921, Einstein actually spent several days at City College, participating in meetings of physicists and philosophers from around the country. On April 14, he spoke to students in the Great Hall at City College, the event my uncle most likely remembered.[2] There's no way of knowing whether Uncle Lou actually jumped on the car's running board, but I never doubted it for a minute.

And yet, even after MIT, Uncle Lou found it hard to get a job in the chemical industry because, it was said, of discrimination against Jews. So Uncle Lou went to work as a chemist for the Federal government in Boston, where he had a successful career. He was frequently in New York for business, and he always made a point of coming to our house in the Bronx for dinner. He took a keen interest in me, especially my schooling, and he was especially pleased when I attended Bronx Science – a kind of successor school to Townsend Harris, which had closed just before World War II.[3] Later, I made sure to visit him from time to time in Boston.

Uncle Lou had become my Einstein.

When our own son, Ned, was born in 1982, we gave him the middle name of Tanner – not just because it was my mother's maiden name but also as a form of homage to my Uncle Lou. He outlived my parents, dying in 1994, a month shy of his 95th birthday. I spoke at his funeral service, and his daughter Marilyn later gave me his MIT diploma, which hangs in my study at home.

Marilyn and I have remained close first cousins over the years. We both knew that the family name had been Tanenzapf, changed to Tanner several years after our grandparents, Benjamin and Millie Tanenzapf, arrived in America in 1904. They came from the East End of London, then a Jewish ghetto, where they had lived for several years.

But the family was originally from a *shtetl* named Kolomaya, in a region called Galicia, in a country that is now Poland. Like nearly all the *shtetls* in Eastern Europe, Kolomaya was later wiped out by the Nazis very early in the war. Marilyn had done some earlier research on the Tanenzapf/Tanner family, and she had sent me some official papers that had been passed on to her.

Among them: a "Petition For Naturalization" in 1912 listing

the Tanenzapf family. All four children were named, including my mother Rachel, known as Ruth, and my Uncle Lou, both born in London, as well as my Aunt Anna, the only child born in Kolomaya, and my Uncle Harry, the only one born in America. By then, they were all living at 9 East 114th Street in Manhattan.

With all this material in hand, I decided to create a family tree, a narrative of the Tanenzapf/Tanner wing of the family. But I knew nothing about Kolomaya or what happened before Benjamin and Millie arrived in America.

At this point, something remarkable happened: In one of those believe-it-or-not coincidences, I had come across a book called *The Tenement Saga: The Lower East Side and Early Jewish American Writers*, written in 2004 by a man named Sanford Sternlicht. I was also familiar with another book he wrote in 2007 – this one called *Masterpieces of Jewish American Literature*.

Sanford Sternlicht? Hmmm. The name sounded familiar. When I was growing up in the Bronx, my mother was friendly with a cousin of hers named Bobbie Sternlicht, who had a son named Sandy, older than I was, who went on to be a writer of some sort. Bobbie died around the same time as my mother in the 1980s, and I lost track of Sandy.

Was this the same guy? Could it be that he too was interested in Jewish-American writers? His books said he was a professor at Syracuse University, and it took just a minute to find his e-mail address on the school's website, where he was listed as Emeritus Professor of English. After some procrastination tinged with the expectant anxiety that comes with opening an old trunk, I wrote him an e-mail that started:

"Sorry for this bolt out of the blue, but I believe we are related."

I went on to explain about my mother and his mother, my interest in Jewish-American writers, a little bit about my life as a journalist, and so on. I finished by saying I would very much welcome a phone conversation and perhaps a meeting at some point. The very next day, I received an e-mail reply that began this way:

"Of course I remember your mother."

After several phone calls and e-mail exchanges over several weeks, he and his wife, Mary Beth Hinton, came to dinner at our apartment in New York. Then 83, Sandy was a tall, soft-spoken, warm man, delighted to reclaim a piece of his past. Not only did he remember my mother, he knew of her brother Lou, the academic superstar. He talked eagerly about the Lower East Side, the Bronx, his family, and the poverty they experienced. His father eked out a living by running a newsstand/candy store, one of those neighborhood places where you could get an egg cream, a legendary fountain drink second only to stickball games in the nostalgic recollection of those of us from the Bronx or Brooklyn.

He told me what he knew about our common roots: He traced our history back to a man named Tanenzapf, first name unknown, who lived in the middle of the 19th century in the Kolomaya *shtetl*, then governed by Austria. He had three children, Benjamin, Bella, and Anne Tanenzapf. Benjamin, in turn, married Millie Zwilich in Kolomaya, and they had four children, including my mother. Several years after emigrating to New York, Benjamin Tanenzapf changed the family name to Tanner.

For her part, Bella had three children, including Sandy's mother, Bobbie. I finally understood my relationship with Sandy: his grandmother Bella and my grandfather Benjamin were brother and sister, making our mothers first cousins. Sandy and I were thus second cousins.

Almost immediately, I called Marilyn to tell her of Sandy, our long-last cousin, and she was delighted to hear the details.

Armed with this new information, I was able to resume work on the family tree, starting in Kolomaya with the man named Tanenzapf, first name unknown. It now spans seven generations forward to my youngest cousins.

Someday, perhaps, I'll see if I can reach farther back into our European past. The Yiddish-speaking culture of Eastern Europe lasted for some 800 years, so there's plenty of history. But life probably didn't change much for the *shtetl*-dwelling ancestors of Mr. Tanenzapf. It might be a better idea to learn as much as I can about Mr. and Mrs. Tanenzapf and their life in Kolomaya.

I want to know how their children decided to emigrate, first to London, and then to New York, how they did it, and what Mr. and Mrs. Tanenzapf thought of the whole cockamamie idea.

Were they too old or too infirm to go with them? How did they accept the almost-certain likelihood that they would never see their three children again? And, by the way, what *were* their first names? At the moment, I have only a recurring fantasy: That Isaac Bashevis Singer would tell their story.

Eight Guys Reading Saul Bellow

In the post-war pantheon of Jewish-American writers, Saul Bellow reigns supreme, the first to crack the WASP hierarchy of American letters, the only novelist to win three National Book Awards, and the first Jewish-American writer to be honored with a Nobel Prize in Literature. Several years ago, I re-read nearly all of his 11 novels, starting with *Dangling Man* (1944) and finishing with *Ravelstein* (2000). I loved three or four of them, but I confess to feeling disappointed by several others. It must be me, I thought. What am I missing that seems so obvious to critics and normal readers alike? So I was delighted when my book group recently decided to read three of Bellow's best-known novels: *The Adventures of Augie March*, *Seize the Day*, and *Herzog*. Finally, another chance to get it.

We chose these three books as representative of the Bellow canon partly because of something that Philip Roth wrote in his 2001 book, *Shop Talk*, which deals with writers and their craft.[1] Roth posited that there are two very different kinds of Bellow novels, with two very distinct Bellow protagonists:

Some of Bellow's books, Roth writes, are "the euphoric-going-every-which-way, out-and-out comic novels, the books that materialize at the very tip-top of the Bellovian mood swing, the merry music of the egosphere that is *Augie March*, *Henderson the Rain King*, and *Humboldt's Gift*..."

By contrast, Roth says, are the "dark, down-in-the-dumps novels, such as *The Victim*, *Seize The Day*, *Mr. Sammler's Planet*, and *The Dean's December*, where the bewildering pain issuing from the heroes' wounds is not taken lightly either by them or by Bellow."

Herzog, published in 1964, is a blend of both the exuberant and the suffering, Roth says. "Herzog strikes me," he writes, "as supreme among Bellow's novels for its magical integration of this characteristic divergence." In praising *Herzog*, Roth hints at his own preference: "It turns out that even more is unlocked in the Bellow hero by suffering than by euphoria." And by combining the two, "he puts the whole Bellovian symphony into play, with its lushly comical orchestration of misery."

Bellow had written two early novels that I liked: *Dangling Man* in 1944 and *The Victim* in 1947, both introspective, both falling into Roth's definition of Bellow's "dark, down-in-the-dumps" novels. *Augie March*, published in 1953, was Bellow's breakthrough novel, an exuberant, over-the-top sensation when it came out. It's hard to imagine that it was written by the same guy.

"I am an American, Chicago born..." Augie proclaims in the book's now-famous first sentence, an opening-bell proclamation that Bellow was determined to shed his immigrant roots and take his place as an American writer right up there with the best. In The Great American Novel sweepstakes, *The Adventures of Augie March* was meant to vie with *The Adventures of Huckleberry Finn*. In one sense, he succeeded. Augie March turned Bellow himself into a breakthrough writer – the first Jew to reach the very top rung of American literature.

Though not religious and opposed to being labeled a Jewish writer, he identified as a Jew throughout his life. He spoke fluent Yiddish, helped make Isaac Bashevis Singer a success by translating *Gimpel the Fool* to English, and regularly spoke out against any hint of anti-Semitism. I always thought of him as a writer who was Jewish, not a writer of Jewish books. And I took pride in his breakthrough.

Augie March is a picaresque novel, a long, adventurous tale in which our roguish hero encounters a series of people of varied sort. Many of them are *gonifs*, ranging from petty crooks to gangsters. There are lost souls, Machiavellian schemers, millionaires, beautiful women, and molls on the make. In this high-low juxtaposition, Bellow paints a marvelous picture of Depression-era Chicago, "that somber city."

Many of the characters, including Augie, are Jewish and some of the dialogue has the cadence of Yiddish, but Augie March is a very American saga. As Philip Roth put it, "You could take the Jew out of the adventurous Augie March without doing much harm to the whole of the book, whereas the same could not be said for taking Chicago out of the boy," he wrote in 1974.[2]

Augie March is also a *bildungsroman*, a coming-of-age story. When we first meet Augie, he is a likeable boy raised by his mother and Grandma Lausch, who is really an unrelated boarder in Augie's desperately poor house but nevertheless rules the roost. He has an older brother Simon and a younger brother Georgie, who is an "idiot," but much loved by Augie. There is no father in sight.

As soon as Augie graduates from high school, he is taken to a brothel for his real commencement. His patron is a family friend, a crippled real-estate shark named Einhorn, who becomes something of a father figure for Augie. If Americans are defined by their work, as Bellow suggests, then Augie is searching "freestyle" for his identity by trying a stunning array of odd jobs, some of them disreputable or downright criminal.

In the course of his odyssey, Augie is a paperboy, a stocker at Woolworth's, a shoe salesman, a butler, a dog-groomer, and a union organizer. He's not above skimming money as a retail clerk or smuggling immigrants in from Canada, and he steals books on demand for college students (though he reads most of them before delivering the hot goods). He falls in love with Thea, who takes him to Mexico to train an eagle to catch lizards. Lest we think the eagle a simple symbol of innocent America, Thea has named the creature Caligula, after the corrupt Roman emperor. Augie enlists in the Merchant Marines during World War II, his ship is torpedoed, and he finds himself floating in a lifeboat with a mad genius before his rescue by a British ship. He ends up marrying a beautiful, aspiring actress named Stella and living in Paris, where he becomes a black-market dealer in Army surplus. Augie, still trying to find himself, remains full of hope.

The novel ends, and the mind reels. At least mine did. I went to the book group wondering how the others felt about *Augie March*. I anticipated that they would like it more than I did, and if so, perhaps I'd learn something from their take.

A word about the book group. I started it in 2014 with my friend, Bert Pogrebin, a lawyer specializing in labor law who had been a friend of Bernard Malamud. We enlisted seven other guys dedicated to the proposition that by reading or re-reading the literary classics we would realize the insights that come with lifelong experience. All of our original recruits were friends of mine or of Bert's: Don Brown, a psychiatrist specializing in family therapy (see Chapter 4 for our Gansevoort Street roots); Victor Navasky, former editor of *The Nation* and professor at the Columbia Journalism School; Sam Norich, the German-born-son of Holocaust survivors, who became the president of *The Forward*; Jack Rosenthal, a former editor at *The New York Times*; Martin Sage, a comedy writer; Herb Teitelbaum, a lawyer; and Jack Willis, a retired documentary film-maker and public-TV producer.

All in all, we're a homogeneous group, older Jewish guys on the verge of retirement or beyond. We joke about our lack of diversity, and perhaps it is true that we are *alte kockers*, desperately in need of the challenging perspective of younger, more diverse members – as I had experienced in auditing the course at City College on Singer. But there's something to be said for a small, homogeneous cohort like ours. In discussing a book, we encounter differences of opinion that may actually be quite revealing precisely because they don't stem from people with diverse backgrounds. Doesn't it mean something if similar people come to different conclusions about a book? Maybe, sometimes, there's something to be gained, as in science, by reducing the number of variables, by minimizing the effects of cultural diversity, whether it's age, gender, ethnicity, or race. In our first three years bonding over books, we've read a wide variety of authors: Ernest Hemingway, William Faulkner, F. Scott Fitzgerald, Virginia Woolf, Mark Twain, Henry Roth, Philip Roth, E.L. Doctorow, James Joyce, George Eliot, James Baldwin, Richard Wright, and Ralph Ellison.[3] Despite our similar backgrounds, we had plenty of disagreements about these writers and their work. We were rarely in lockstep. One more thing we discovered about ourselves: Our robust discussions were conducted with a civility that might have been absent if we were talking about, say, politics or the Middle East, subjects in which we all thought ourselves expert. When it came to literature, we were more humble. None of us had a PhD in comp lit.

And so, one chilly March evening, we shuttled to the Brooklyn Heights apartment of Sam Norich to launch into Saul Bellow's *Augie March*. There were eight of us, Jack Willis having dropped out for health reasons. Much to my surprise, the group was uniformly disappointed in the novel. They didn't like it any more than I did.

Jack Rosenthal, always soft-spoken, nonetheless started the discussion in blunt fashion: "I confess that I was unimpressed," he said. The novel felt like a "series of short stories strung together." It was episodic, not a sustained narrative, he thought, and Augie "never really defines himself."

Herb Teitelbaum quickly agreed. "I counted 70 characters, including Caligula, the eagle. I couldn't keep track of all of them." Worse, he concluded, "Augie didn't grow very much," a verdict seconded by Victor Navasky. But Victor thought the ending, though just another episode, was appropriate. "It was a reaffirmation of what he was."

Playing devil's advocate, I piped up: "Maybe it's more realistic for a character not to grow in a dramatically satisfying way." I found no takers.

We were quickly forming a consensus: If the book is a coming-of-age story, why doesn't Augie grow into a man who understands himself? How much do all those encounters really change him? After nearly 600 pages, he is not much closer to self-knowledge or finding his place in the world than he was when we first met him.

So what was all the shouting about in 1953? Curious, I downloaded some early reviews. Some of the critics had significant reservations, including Robert Gorham Davis, who reviewed *Augie* on the front page of the *New York Times Book Review*: "A series of events do not make a dramatic whole just because they happen to one man, and if a man's life seems to have an underlying pattern, the man himself is not usually the one best able to discern it." [4]

And what of the comparison to *Huckleberry Finn*? Yes, Huck is also a picaresque hero, a charming rebel who encounters all sorts of characters on his way down the Mississippi, and those vignettes help shape him. But the centerpiece of *Huckleberry Finn* is Huck's poignant relationship to Jim, the runaway slave. There's no such deep, endearing relationship in *Augie March*.

There is plenty of sex, much adventure, and many colorful people, but in the end they are just a series of encounters.

Joan Acocella, writing in *The New Yorker* in 2003, on the 50th anniversary of the publication of *Augie March*, sees it as a pioneering triumph by Bellow, but offers some reservations that I share: [5]

"The novel runs out of steam in its last quarter or so, but that is often the case with a bildungsroman...because it is the quest that is romantic, and no ending of that, no fall into adult life, will seem a worthy conclusion."

Though our book group found consensus about the overall story, we bickered about Bellow's flowery writing style and whether his obvious erudition was often pedantic, as in the frequent references to the likes of Seneca, Plato, Cincinnatus, Alcibiades, Rousseau, and Sardanapalus. Both Bert Pogrebin and Sam Norich enjoyed much of the poetic language, the rich cascading sentences full of vivid descriptions. In effect, they were echoing what critic Joan Acocella wrote about Bellow's sentences: "They are like hall closets; you open them and everything falls out." But Jack Rosenthal deemed Bellow's prose "grandiose and over-written." Bellow, he said, was "showing off." As exhibit A, he read aloud the first paragraph of Chapter 11:

"Now there's a dark Westminster of a time when a multitude of objects cannot be clear; they're too dense and there's an island rain, North Sea lightlessness, the vein of the Thames. That darkness, in which resolutions have to be made – it isn't merely local; it's the same darkness that exists in the fiercest clearnesses of torrid Medina. And what about the coldness of the rain? That doesn't deheat foolishness in its residence of the human face, nor take away deception nor change defects, but this rain is an emblem of the shared condition of all. It maybe means that what is needed to mitigate the foolishness or dissolve the deception is always superabundantly about and insistently offered to us – a black offer in Charing Cross; a gray in Place Pereires where you see so many kinds and varieties of beings going to and fro in the liquid and fog; a brown in the straight unity of Wabash Avenue. With the dark, the solvent is in this way offered until the time when one thing is determined and the offers, mercies, and opportunities are finished."

The passage is hard going, over-ripe with obscure allusion. Having re-read it several times, I agree with Jack Rosenthal's assessment. It does feels as if Bellow is showboating.[6]

We moved on to *Seize The Day*, a short novel published in 1956, just three years after *Augie March*, but radically different. It is barely over 100 pages, so brief that the original hardcover edition contained three other stories and even a one-act play. Alfred Kazin, praising it in the *New York Times*, called *Seize The Day* "a novel in miniature," [7] and V.S. Pritchett, the noted British critic, called it "a small grey masterpiece." [8] It is also a gray book, in Roth's sense of "dark and down-in-the dumps."

Seize The Day is the day of reckoning for Tommy Wilhelm (nee Adler), who has hit rock bottom. At 44, he has no job, no money, no hope. His father, a retired doctor, shows little compassion or love for his son, vehemently refusing to give him a dime to help pay his bills. His estranged wife, Margaret, denies him the divorce he craves, while upping her demands for bigger child support payments. Wilhelm is isolated and desperate. Through flashbacks and interior monologues, we learn how he came to this bleak pass. He dropped out of Penn State as a sophomore, after a phony talent scout named Maurice Venice played on his fantasy of becoming a movie star. He went to Hollywood for seven years, but managed nothing more than minor roles as an extra. He returned to New York, worked as a sales executive, married, and had two sons. But he lost it all and moved into the Hotel Gloriana, a Broadway hostel for elderly Jews on the Upper West Side, where his father, now widowed, also lives. Wilhelm comes under the spell of a con man named Tampkin, a quack psychologist who cheats Wilhelm of his remaining money by promising to make a bundle in the commodities market by investing in lard.

The novel ends in stunning fashion. Broke, fevered, and despairing, Wilhelm wanders along Broadway, only to find himself in a chapel during a funeral for a man, a stranger to him, who lies in an open coffin. Catching sight of the man, Wilhelm suddenly erupt in tears and sobs, a crying spell so intense and uncontrollable that the mourners speculate that he must be a close relative – perhaps the cousin from New Orleans they were expecting, or even the man's brother. It's a powerful climax, emotional and mysterious.

Our book group, meeting in Martin Sage's apartment in Greenwich Village, couldn't wait to weigh in. Herb Teitelbaum opened by neatly describing Wilhelm's inner struggle – how he abdicates all responsibility for himself, blames others for his problems, and relinquishes his freedom by seeking solace from con men like Venice and Tampkin. He becomes marginalized, living on the periphery. As in Hollywood, he is reduced to being an extra.

All of us agreed with Herb's take on Wilhelm. And we acknowledged that Tamkin, for all his phony conniving, offered a kernel of existential truth when he advised Wilhelm to forget the past as well as the prospect of some future salvation: "Only the present is real – the here and now. Seize the day."

The novel's dramatic ending in the funeral chapel, however, was unconvincing to both Sam Norich and Bert Pogrebin. Sam didn't see any great change in Wilhelm, any deep moment of truth. He was merely grieving for himself, more pathetic than tragic. Bert agreed, calling Wilhelm an "empty character," and arguing, lawyer-like, that there was no evidence of any change in Wilhelm. Victor Navasky split the difference. He felt that Wilhelm experienced a "genuinely emotional moment," but it was unclear whether he would change as a result. Herb added that it was not necessary for Bellow to tell what subsequently happens to Wilhelm.

Bellow's aim, I thought, was to portray an ordinary man and find compassion for him. In my view, the ending was cathartic for Wilhelm, enabling him to find his grief for the first time, to connect at last with himself and thus to the larger world. Sam disagreed, with good humor, calling my view wishful thinking: "the triumph of hope over experience."

Maybe, I laughed. But I felt vindicated when Don Brown offered a psychoanalytic interpretation for the final scene, which he deemed a "breakthrough" for Wilhelm, a shift in his perception, enabling him, potentially at least, to take responsibility for himself. "People can't move on," Don said, "unless they grieve and open themselves to their emotions." Neither Sam nor Bert seemed persuaded.

"Imagine losing your spouse after 40 years," Don continued. "What is the healthy way to move on? By grieving. By experiencing the pain. By touching the sadness." Only then, he said, can you see the potential for transcending grief. Don thought the image of the corpse in the novel's final scene was important: "Seeing a dead body made Wilhelm understand that life is finite." All the more reason, he said, to seize the day.

We were now ready for the third book on our Bellow reading list, *Herzog*, published in 1964. In reading *Herzog* right after *Seize The Day*, I was immediately struck by certain similarities between the protagonists of each novel: Moses Herzog and Tommy Wilhelm. Both are Jewish men in their mid-40s who are going through a mid-life crisis. Both are haunted by difficulties with estranged wives. Both fear losing touch with their children. Both have girlfriends who present problems. Both, to different degrees and in different ways, are failures at work. And both experience moments of epiphany – not exactly happy endings, but at least a hint of transcendence suggesting better days ahead. There are, of course, major differences between Herzog and Wilhelm, but I couldn't help wondering about Bellow's focus on middle-aged men in crisis.

The protagonist of *Herzog* – the "hero-patsy," as Irving Howe calls him,[9] is an academic who wrote a scholarly book called "*Romanticism and Christianity*," but has been unable to write anything else, including his unfinished PhD thesis. Instead, he writes letters – to himself, to friends, mistresses, his psychiatrist, fellow academics, as well as famous people throughout history, including Eisenhower, Nietzsche, Adlai Stevenson, Martin Luther King, and the physicist Erwin Schrodinger. Naturally, he never sends any of them. The letters are Bellow's way of expressing his own philosophical musings, as well as Herzog's inner thoughts. Herzog is obsessed, among other things, by beautiful women and sex, by being Jewish in WASP America, by his two failed marriages, and by the risk of losing his children. He thinks about the meaning of life, the meaning of death, all against the twin horrors of his lifetime that lurk in the background: the Depression and the Holocaust.

Herzog's immediate crisis concerns his second wife, the beautiful, Radcliffe-educated Madeleine, who is portrayed by Herzog as the ultimate ball-breaking bitch who "eats green salads and drinks human blood." She converted from Judaism to Catholicism soon after college and is now pursuing a PhD at Fordham University. She is also the mother of his second child, June. Above all else is the fact, known to all, that Madeleine cuckolded Herzog by taking up with his best friend, Valentine Gersbach, who has left his own wife for Madeleine. Gersbach has a wooden leg and poles himself along, Herzog says, "like a gondolier" in Venice. Madeleine and Gersbach now live together in Chicago with June, Herzog's young daughter.

Herzog gets it in his head that June is in danger from Gersbach, and resolves to go to Chicago, kill Gersbach, and rescue June. He takes a loaded antique pistol from his late father's desk, where it is wrapped in rubles from the Czarist era, and heads to Chicago. When he arrives, he secretly watches Gersbach giving June a bath, with obvious tenderness and affection. Despite his fevered state, Herzog realizes June is in no danger at all. Now worried that he will lose June's love, he takes her on a father-daughter trip to the aquarium, but crashes his car and gets arrested, charged with carrying a loaded gun.

He is bailed out by his brother Will and retreats to his dilapidated farmhouse in the Berkshires, on "the edge of nowhere," where owls roost in the bedroom and dead birds litter the toilet bowl. And yet Herzog finds tranquility in his farmhouse, which he vows to fix up. He seems to reject the intellectual life in favor of rural calm.

Herzog is soon visited by his girlfriend, a ravishing Argentinian Jewess, a sexpot named Ramona, who wants to marry him. Herzog is ambivalent, leery of entering a third marriage. As he prepares to cook dinner for her, a serenity comes over him, an inner peace. The book ends with Herzog vowing to stop writing any more letters. "At this time, he thinks to himself, "he had no messages for anyone. Nothing. Not a single word."

But there's no real resolution, and I was left wondering just why Herzog achieved such a release from the angst that plagued him during the entire novel.

What did others in our book group think?

Bert Pogrebin felt Herzog's ambivalence was mainly an internal struggle between his desire for revenge against Madeleine and Gersbach, on the one hand, and his understanding of their wish for personal happiness, on the other hand. He didn't buy the idea that Herzog's ambivalence dissipated by the end or that he found an inner peace that would somehow last. Neither did most of the others in the group. "There were many interesting ideas along the way," Victor Navasky said, "but no real resolution."

Only Don Brown, our resident shrink, thought that the ending brought some clarity. He thought that Herzog was much less nihilistic than Tommy Wilhelm, and showed signs of moving on from his rage against Madeleine and Gersbach. Far from living in an existential void, as Wilhelm did, Herzog had good friends, a sympathetic brother, and a girlfriend. Even when he sees Gersbach bathing June, he is able to appreciate Gersbach's love for the child.

At the end, in the Berkshire farmhouse, when the caretaker, Mrs. Tuttle, overhears conversations revealing Herzog's embarrassment, she seems unfazed, a further signal to Herzog to accept the situation, give up his quest for some sort of justice, and find happiness, perhaps with Ramona. Some of us also found reason for optimism when Herzog decided to stop writing all those letters to everybody. "He was no longer using an intellectual outlet to hide his emotional pain," Don suggested.

Whereas *Seize the Day* ends with an emotional bang, *Herzog* ends with an existential whimper. Either way, there's some sort of resolution, Bellow style.

Some critics see an Old Testament interpretation. In his biography of Bellow, Zachary Leader[10] points out that Herzog, sitting in his farmhouse, says to himself, "*Hineni*," using the Hebrew word for "here I am." "How beautiful it is today." Leader tells us that *Hineni* is the word of acceptance uttered by

Abraham just before God commands him to sacrifice his son Isaac (a test of faith later withdrawn). In *Herzog*, says Leader, it signals Herzog's acceptance not only of his situation but also of his faith in something radiant in place of Abraham's God. He achieves a sense of inner calm, a solace in spirituality in lieu of an intellectual life.

Is *Herzog* a "Jewish" book? Herb thought so: "It's all about Jews," he said, starting with the arrival in America of Herzog's family and his father's struggle to earn a living. Those are common themes in immigrant literature, but here applied to Jews. Jack Rosenthal, who thought the book "pedantic," said he was nonetheless moved by the descriptions of Herzog's father, an impoverished peddler and bootlegger in Montreal's Jewish quarter. And, as Don stressed, Herzog can be seen as a symbol of the landless Jew who finds comfort in a piece of land in rural America. It's only a rundown farmhouse in the Berkshires, but it seems to trigger some sort of conversion, religious or otherwise, in our weary hero.

Overall, like others in our group, I ended up with mixed feelings about Saul Bellow. I realized I much prefer when he focuses, up close and personal, on the psychological drama of a man in turmoil, rather than the episodic sprawl of the picaresque. So I loved *Seize The Day*, but I was less moved by *Augie March*, a man without a narrative. *Herzog* is somewhere in the middle, a comic probe into a damaged man, a terrific book marred somewhat by Bellow's pedantry. Now that I think about it, I felt the same way about the Bellow books I had read earlier: Thumbs up for such introspective novels as *The Victim* and *Mr. Sammler's Planet*, misgivings about the more sprawling books, like *Henderson the Rain King* and *Humboldt's Gift*. I found myself wondering why Bellow had won a Nobel Prize, while Philip Roth hasn't. At least not yet.

NINE

Literary
Anti-Semitism

In the years following Saul Bellow's ascension, Jews emerged as major writers of novels, short stories, plays, and criticism, creating a new hierarchy in American letters. And guess what? Old prejudices re-surfaced, this time in the upper precincts of American literature. The WASP establishment, or at least some of it, felt excluded from the new literary order, and took to complaining about the merits of some Jewish writing in ways that were anti-Semitic. "I felt that many writers treated their Jewish colleagues with unpardonable shabbiness," said Bellow. "Some people were saying there was a Jewish mafia, and other people – well, they didn't use the word conspiracy, but they saw it as an unwelcome eruption." [1]

Bellow and others thought that the very category of "Jewish-American writer" was itself a form of discrimination, a way of ghettoizing them, of denying them any universal appeal beyond the strictly parochial. "When most people call you a

'Jewish writer,' it's a way of setting you aside," he said.[2]

Bellow was especially sensitive to any slight, stemming in part from the anti-Semitism he experienced as a boy in Montreal.[3] Beyond the obvious Jewish stereotypes of Shakespeare's Shylock or Dickens' Fagin, Bellow could quote anti-Jewish sentences in the writing of T.S. Eliot, Ezra Pound, and Henry James, and he was well aware of the casual anti-Semitism in Hemingway, Fitzgerald, and Thomas Wolfe.[4] He was angered by the failure of Edmund Wilson to review any of his books after his first novel, *Dangling Man*, was published in 1944 – further evidence, he said, of "the whole WASP effort to suppress the Jewish novel."[5]

Bellow's complaint was underscored by the words of Katherine Anne Porter, Truman Capote, and Gore Vidal. Porter, author of the fine novel, *Ship of Fools*, as well as many brilliant short stories and novellas, including one of my favorites, *Noon Wine*, revealed her colors in an interview with *Harper's* magazine in September 1965. Toward the end of a long Q&A, she let loose a no-holds-barred attack on Jewish writers and critics, "a crowd with headquarters in New York," especially their use of the English language.[6]

Citing her deep Southern roots, Porter claimed a special legitimacy in using English as the mother tongue: "We do not abuse it or misuse it, and when we speak a word, we know what it means." By contrast, she said, "these others have fallen into a curious kind of argot, more or less originating in New York, a deadly mixture of academic, guttersnipe, gangster, fake-Yiddish, and dull old worn-out dirty words." Their writing," she said, shows "an appalling bankruptcy in language, as if they hate English and are trying to destroy *it along with all other livings things they touch* [italics added]." [7]

Three years later, Truman Capote, another Southern writer (pardon the expression), picked up his musket in an interview in the March 1968 issue of *Playboy* magazine, complaining of "the rise of...the Jewish Mafia in American letters..." [8] Here it is verbatim:

"This is a clique of New York-oriented writers and critics who control much of the literary scene through the influence of the quarterlies and intellectual magazines. All these publications are Jewish dominated...and this particular coterie employs them to make or break writers by advancing or withholding attention. Bernard Malamud, and Saul Bellow, and Philip Roth, and Isaac Bashevis Singer, and Norman Mailer are all fine writers but they are not the only writers in the country, as the Jewish literary Mafia would have us believe." [9]

Gore Vidal, never to be outdone, joined the fray in a 1970 essay in, of all places, *Commentary* magazine, then published by the American Jewish Committee. Vidal echoed Porter's complaint about "immigrant" English: "With each generation American prose grows worse, reflecting confused thinking, poor education, and the incomplete assimilation of immigrant English into the old language." [10]

Vidal went on to attack several prominent critics, all of them Jewish, including Richard Gilman, John Simon, and Robert Brustein. They are all "literary gangsters," he wrote, "hit-

and-run journalists, without conscience, forced to live precariously by their wits, and those wits are increasingly strained these days because there are fewer places to publish…which means a lot more edgy hoods hanging about the playgrounds of the West Side." [11]

It's surreal to read such comments today. Whether blatant or disguised in code words, the anti-Semitism from some of our best-known writers was delivered without embarrassment, as if no one could possibly think otherwise. As Walter Cronkite might have said, "And that's the way it was."

I was never much of a fan of Gore Vidal, but I did admire the work of Katherine Anne Porter and Truman Capote. Having discovered their charged comments only recently, I feel betrayed. How can I continue to enjoy their fiction? Perhaps I should just chalk it up to the temper of the times. Or separate the art from the artist, the way music lovers do when they listen to Wagner.

Maybe it doesn't matter any longer. I'm not sure, however, that I can simply move on. I just don't feel the same way about them or, at the moment, their writing.

TEN

Philip Roth's Turning Point

Philip Roth is one of those rare writers who got better with age. He turned out some of his best novels when he was in his 60s, including such masterpieces as *Sabbath's Theater, American Pastoral*, and *The Human Stain*, as well as his last book, the moving short novel, *Nemesis*, written when he was 77. His career has been so long and productive that it is hard to remember how uneven his books were in his first 20 years as a novelist.

He burst on the literary scene in 1959, at age 26, with a few short stories and *Goodbye, Columbus*, a witty and touching novella that satirized *nouveau riche* Jews in suburban New Jersey – and caused a fuss among some Jews who didn't like what they saw as dirty linen aired in public. His next two novels misfired, dismissed by critics and readers alike.[1] It wasn't until a decade later, in 1969, that he hit it big with *Portnoy's Complaint*, a riot of a novel about a sexually exuberant young man and his Jewish mother, to put it mildly. It caused an even bigger stir, and

Roth got rich and famous, a notorious bad boy. But his next five novels proved disappointing,[2] and by 1979, when he was 46, he could claim only two important books – "not a sterling record," says Claudia Roth Pierpont in her insightful literary biography, *Roth Unbound*, published in 2013. "Roth's literary future was, at best, uncertain," she wrote.[3]

Then in 1979, he wrote a short novel, *The Ghost Writer*, which proved to be a turning point in his career. First published in *The New Yorker* in two parts, the book was released a couple of months later to strong reviews. It was a finalist for the National Book Award in 1980, and the Pulitzer Prize jury voted to give it the fiction award, only to be overruled by the Pulitzer board, which instead chose *The Executioner's Song*, by Norman Mailer.[4] From her vantage point nearly 35 years later, Pierpont waxes rhapsodic about *The Ghost Writer*. "From the opening paragraph," she says, "one feels a new calm and lucid power in the writing." She even likens it to *The Great Gatsby*, calling *The Ghost Writer* "one of our literature's rare and nearly perfect books."[5]

High praise, and I certainly agree that *The Ghost Writer* was a splendid book for Roth, and a re-routing of his career. It was the first time he deployed Nathan Zuckerman as a first-person narrator who served as his alter ego (though Zuckerman had briefly appeared in an earlier book). To Roth, Zuckerman was a disguise, like wearing a mask, that freed Roth to let go in a way he hadn't since *Portnoy's Complaint*, to write with the energetic voice and ironic tone that were his trademarks. "I am your permission...your indiscretion," the fictional Zuckerman tells the real Roth in *The Facts*, Roth's early memoir.[6]

Roth tapped Zuckerman as an alter ego in eight more novels after *The Ghost Writer*.[7] Roth said he was "fictionalizing himself...coaxing into existence a being whose experience was comparable to my own and yet registered a more powerful valence, a life more highly charged and energized, more entertaining than my own."[8]

The Ghost Writer, via Nathan Zuckerman, finally allowed Roth to deal with the charges that had plagued him from his earliest work – namely that he was a self-hating Jew who gave aid and comfort to anti-Semites by dwelling on the foibles and shortcomings of American Jews. The backlash had started with one of his first short stories, *Defender of the Faith*, that ran in *The New Yorker* in April 1959 and was included a month later in the *Goodbye, Columbus* volume.

Defender of the Faith deals with a conflict between two Jews, both soldiers during the waning days of World War 2. Sergeant Nathan Marx, a war hero, has returned from Germany after the defeat of the Nazis to train a group of new recruits for possible service in the remaining fight against the Japanese. One of them, 19-year-old Sheldon Grossbard, is as conniving and disagreeable as Sergeant Marx is upright and likeable. Playing on their shared Jewishness in a Christian environment, Grossbard seeks favors from Marx, routinely lying along the way, and culminating in a selfish ploy to avoid being sent to the Pacific theater. Marx, traumatized by the devastation he saw in Europe and conscious of his own Jewish roots, engages in soul-searching before undermining Grossbard's dishonest scheme to avoid overseas service. Grossbard reacts by calling Marx an anti-Semite.

The fallout from the story was swift. How could Grossbard, a Jew, a soldier in wartime no less, behave in such a despicable way? Never mind the exemplary behavior of the Jewish sergeant, a real *mensch*, or his heart-felt struggle to do the right thing, to defend the faith of honesty and fairness. Just 14 years after the Holocaust – 5,000 days – Grossbard wasn't good for the Jews. What would the goyim say?

But it was mainly Jews who had plenty to say. "An eminent New York rabbi," as Roth describes him, wrote a letter to the Anti-Defamation League protesting the story and its 26-year-old author. "What is being done to stop this man?" the rabbi wanted to know. Two representatives of the ADL soon had lunch with Roth, but the meeting was amicable, with nary a warning to Roth about what he should or shouldn't write. "They told me that they had wanted to meet me only to let me know about the complaints... and answer any questions I might have," Roth wrote in *The Facts*. "I figured, however, that a part of their mission was also to see whether I was a nut...In the atmosphere of easy going civility that had been established among us over lunch, I said as much, and we all laughed." [9]

It was no laughing matter to some others, however, especially after *Goodbye, Columbus* was published. Satirizing the class divide among certain assimilated Jews in New Jersey, Roth tells the tale of Brenda Patimkin and her romance with Neil Klugman. Brenda is a pretty Radcliffe student from a wealthy suburban family well practiced in the fine art of conspicuous consumption, the money coming from the family business, Patimkin Kitchen and Bathroom Sinks. Neil is an earnest guy from the other side of the Jewish tracks – a graduate of the

Newark campus of Rutgers University who works at the main desk of the Newark Public Library.

When *Goodbye, Columbus* was published, I was a junior at the City College of New York, and the book reverberated on a campus not so different from the Newark branch of Rutgers. CCNY, always a working-class school, was the alma mater of several leading Jewish-American writers and literary critics, including Henry Roth, Bernard Malamud, Paddy Chayefsky, Alfred Kazin, and Irving Howe. The student body was still largely Jewish in my day, and I can remember much discussion of Philip Roth's take on the Jews. Not surprisingly, most of us identified with Neil – the outsider, the underdog, the striver, the critic. The book squared so well with my own sense of things Jewish, which wasn't very different than Roth's, who was only a few years older. More than Bellow or Malamud, Roth felt like my contemporary, writing about my issues, my longings, my concerns. And, of course, sex. I became a Roth fan, reading every novel as soon as it came out – thrilled by some, disappointed by others.

In the larger world, *Goodbye, Columbus* gathered strong reviews, gained high praise from Roth's literary elders (including Saul Bellow), and won the National Book Award in 1960. *Goodbye, Columbus*, wrote scholar Michael Rothberg, was "a lampooning of the suburbanization and 'whitening' of American Jews during the increasingly prosperous 1950s." [10]

But some Jews saw it as nasty stereotyping that would only encourage anti-Semitism. In an interview with the *New York Post*, Leon Uris, author of Exodus, a best-seller published a year earlier, blasted away. "There is a whole school of Jewish writers, who spend their time damning their fathers, hating their mothers, wringing their hands...This isn't art or literature...Their work is obnoxious and makes me sick to my stomach." [11] Uris didn't name Roth, but he didn't have to.

In 1962, Roth accepted an invitation to appear on a panel at Yeshiva University in New York, along with others, including Ralph Ellison, author of *Invisible Man*, a distinguished novel about black life in America. The panel was supposed to discuss minority writers of fiction, but it soon turned into an inquisition of Roth. The moderator's first question: "Mr. Roth, would you write the same stories you've written if you were living in Nazi Germany?" [12]

Roth was grilled for 30 minutes: "I realized that I was not just opposed but hated," he later wrote.[13] Ellison, who had experienced similar criticism from some African-Americans after *Invisible Man*, jumped to Roth's defense, but Roth was dazed. Afterwards, eating a pastrami sandwich at the Stage Delicatessen, Roth was ashamed about his own poor performance and still angry about the questions. "I'll never write about Jews again," he asserted.[14]

But never again never happened. Quite the opposite. "I couldn't see then," Roth later said, "that the most brutal public exchange of my life constituted not the end of my imagination's involvement with the Jews...but the real beginning of my thralldom." [15]

It took him a while to rejoin the fray. Tormented by a disastrous marriage to Maggie Williams, a divorced woman who had two young children, Roth spun his wheels. He wrote two weak novels after *Goodbye, Columbus*, including one that tried to expunge the trauma he felt over his failed marriage.[16] Then came *Portnoy's Complaint*, which took Roth back to his familiar turf with a notorious bang. "My Jewish detractors... wouldn't let up...So I thought finally, 'Well, you want it, I'll give it to you.' And out came Portnoy, apertures spurting."[17]

Portnoy is Alexander Portnoy, a 33-year-old lawyer for the "City of New York Commission on Human Opportunity," and the entire novel plays out on a psychiatrist's couch in the office of a Freudian named Dr. Spielvogel. The psychoanalytic conceit allows Roth full freedom to have Portnoy say outrageous things, using whatever dirty language comes to mind. It's all one hilarious Jewish joke: the beleaguered father, the domineering mother, the ambitious son struggling to break free, the sexual acting out of compulsive masturbation, and ultimately the desire to molt from Jewish boy to American man, expressed in the *shiksa* fantasy of seducing every blond woman he meets. "What I'm saying, Doctor, is that I don't seem to stick my dick up these girls, as much as I stick it up their backgrounds – as though through fucking I will discover America."

As if that wasn't enough to inflame Jewish opinion, Portnoy tells Dr. Spielvogel of a trip to Israel that turns into a disaster when he tries to fuck a Sabra goddess in the holy land ("open wide that messianic Jewish hole"), only to become impotent.

Yet, for all the sexual obsession, for all the parody and farce, Roth also captured the look and feel of lower-middle class Jewish life in the 1940s and 1950s – full of the fear, the hunkered-down Jewishness, and the poignance I remember so well myself.

No surprise, the book was a runaway hit, out-racing *The*

Godfather as the number one best seller of 1969. (Apparently, ethnic profiling, whether of a Jewish mama's boy or of Italian gangsters, was having a very good year.) But *Portnoy's Complaint* made Roth *persona non grata* in certain quarters, especially when a movie version of *Goodbye, Columbus* was released two months after *Portnoy's Complaint* was published. In an ironic twist, it was the movie of *Goodbye, Columbus*, not the original book, that depicted the most egregious stereotypes of Jews, including the over-the-top wedding party when Brenda Patimkin's brother got married.[18]

Commentary, published by the American Jewish Committee, was particularly offended by *Portnoy's Complaint*. Its reviewer, Peter Shaw, attacked the book for "fanaticism in the hatred of things Jewish."[19] Irving Howe, in condemning *Portnoy's Complaint*, withdrew his earlier praise of *Goodbye, Columbus*. And Norman Podhoretz, the magazine's editor, went after Roth's overall reputation.[20] Even the *New York Times* ranted against the book for its "revolting sexual excesses" in an editorial on April 1, 1969, headlined "Beyond the (Garbage) Pale," ignoring the high praise by its own book reviewer.[21]

Roth had his own take on all the fuss, noting that a Jew is supposed to act with decorum and restraint, not go wild in public. "He is not expected to make a spectacle of himself, either by shooting off his mouth or by shooting off his semen, and certainly not by shooting off his mouth about shooting off his semen."[22]

Roth, of course, had the last laugh. *Portnoy's Complaint* has continued to shine in the literary firmament, even as other once-lauded books of the same era lost their luster, including

John Updike's *Couples*, a sexually explicit story of suburban wife-swapping published about the same time. In 1998, the Modern Library ranked *Portnoy's Complaint* number 52 on its list of the 100 best English-language novels of the 20th century. And in 2005 *Time* magazine named *Portnoy's Complaint* to its top 100 list of English-language novels published since 1923.[23]

But the book's notoriety all but paralyzed Roth. He sent his parents on a month-long trip to Europe and Israel to escape the storm he knew was coming, and he himself retreated to Yaddo, the writer's colony that would serve as his temporary witness-protection-program. He did write five more novels over the next eight years, but none of them, Pierpont wrote, "did his reputation much good." The books were, she said, "a reflection of his post-Portnoy uncertainty and confusion."[24]

What was he confused about? Much of it had to do with his lingering anger about Maggie, his ex-wife, especially how she tricked him into marrying her by faking a pregnancy with a phony urine sample. He just couldn't seem to get it out of his head, so much so that six years after her death in an automobile accident, he wrote yet another novel attempting to deal with it, *My Life as a Man*, published in 1974. The character is called Maureen Tarnopol, and everything about the saga of Maggie that was eating at Roth is here, including the fake pregnancy and urine sample. The book drew mixed reviews, but whatever its merits as a novel, it seems to have freed Roth, at last, from the crippling trauma of his first marriage and its aftermath.

The stage was now set, finally, for Roth's turnaround novel in 1979, *The Ghost Writer*, the beginning of his extraordinary run to the top ranks of American literature. The story unfolds on a wintery night in 1956, when 23-year-old Nathan Zuckerman goes to the rural Massachusetts home of E.I. Lonoff, a distinguished writer modeled after Bernard Malamud. An aspiring writer with four short stories to his credit, Nathan is looking for Lonoff to be his mentor and his spiritual father, to win, "if I could, the magical protection of his advocacy and his love."

Lonoff is portrayed as living an idealized writer's life, "the most famous literary ascetic in America," a man dedicated to his art to the exclusion of everything else. "I turn sentences around," Lonoff says. "That's my life. I write a sentence and then turn it around. Then I look at it and I turn it around again. Then I have lunch. Then I come back in and write another sentence. Then I have tea and turn the new sentence around. Then I read the two sentences over and turn them both around. Then I lie down on my sofa and think..."

Lonoff's long-suffering wife – named Hope – is fed up with his single-minded devotion to writing and his rejection of her. "*Not* living is what he makes beautiful fiction out of," she complains. But to Nathan, Lonoff's life is literary nirvana.

The Ghost Writer is about many things dear to Roth (and Malamud), especially the importance of literature and the sacrifices it takes to write fiction that matters. Lonoff is taken up by the "religion of art," or as Henry James calls it in a passage Lonoff tapes to the wall above his desk: "the madness of art." Roth later incorporated *The Ghost Writer* into a trilogy called *Zuckerman Bound*, which deals extensively with writers and writing.

But Roth is never far from the Jewish themes that concern him. Nathan Zuckerman is at odds with his own father, a foot doctor, who disapproves of Nathan's forthcoming short story, which depicts Jews in an unflattering fight over money – as if Jews were somehow exempt from the foibles of human nature.[25] Nathan's father asks a family friend, Judge Leopold Wapter, to intervene, and Judge Wapter then sends Nathan a letter asking him the very same question Roth was asked at the infamous panel at Yeshiva University in 1962: "If you had been living in Nazi Germany in the 1930s, would you have written such a story?" For good measure, the good judge urges Nathan to see a play he himself had just seen on Broadway: *The Diary of Anne Frank*.

It just so happens that there's a 26-year old woman visiting the Lonoff house at the same time as Nathan, an attractive researcher from Harvard who was once a former student of Lonoff's, as well as his ex-mistress. Her name is Amy Bellette, and her European background is mysterious. When Nathan asks Lonoff about her accent, he replies, "That is from the country of Fetching."

We soon hear that Amy has told a fantastic story to Lonoff: that she is really Anne Frank, that she survived the concentration camps after her family was found hiding in an attic in Amsterdam, that she lived with a foster family in England for three years, that she came to America as just another refugee from Nazi tyranny, that she kept her identity secret because she knew a living person could not be a symbol of Jewish suffering or a martyr for a just cause.

If her famous diary, published in 1947, were known to be

the work of a living writer, Roth writes, it would never be more than a "young teenager's diary of her trying years in hiding during the German occupation of Holland, something boys and girls could read in bed at night along with the adventures of the Swiss Family Robinson." But dead, Roth continues, "she had something more to offer than amusement for ages 10-15; dead she had written, without meaning to or trying to, a book with the force of a masterpiece to make people finally see."

Roth's storytelling is so detailed and emotionally wrenching that I found myself fantasizing, despite everything I knew, that Amy's far-fetched tale was true. I wanted to suspend disbelief.

But not for long. It turns out that Nathan Zuckerman has imagined the whole story of Amy as Anne. And why? Because he seeks a way to make everything all right with his father, as well as Judge Wapter and all the like-minded Jews of the world. "I met a marvelous young woman while I was up in New England," Nathan imagines himself saying to his parents in New Jersey. "I love her and she loves me. We are going to be married."

"Married? But so fast? Nathan, is she Jewish?"

"Yes, she is."

"But who is she?"

"Anne Frank."

..."Anne – the Anne? Oh, how I have misunderstood my son. How mistaken we have been!"

In concocting the novel, with Anne as the ghost haunting us all and Nathan as the ghostwriter re-imagining her story for his own purposes, Roth has serious themes in mind. He notes

that Anne and her family were assimilated Jews, barely observant of Jewish religious practices. "...once a year the Franks
sang a harmless Chanukah song, said some Hebrew words,
lighted some candles, exchanged some presents – a ceremony
lasting about ten minutes – and that was all it took to make
them the enemy. It did not even take that much. It took nothing – that was the horror."

In fictionalizing a polemic point, Roth is telling his critics
that it simply doesn't work for Jews to behave "correctly" –
not too Jewish, not too concerned about money, not too aggressive, and so on. Jews do not cause anti-Semitism, Roth is
saying. Anti-Semites cause anti-Semitism. Period. In *The Ghost
Writer*, Roth made the case, as artfully as he knew how – an
argument that had eluded him 17 years earlier on the panel at
Yeshiva University.

By evoking Anne Frank, Roth also shows his concern over
"the unbridgeable distance between the Holocaust and American life," says scholar Michael Rothberg. As he did in *Eli, The
Fanatic*, Roth "explores the riddles of a history that could si-
multaneously produce unprecedented wealth and success on
one shore and unprecedented destruction on another." [26]

What American Jew of my generation didn't ask himself the
same searing question implicitly raised by Roth: Why them
and not me? Perhaps that's why I was mesmerized when I saw
the photos of victims at Buchenwald when the full horror was
finally revealed to the world. There but for the grace of God
go I. Grace? What grace? God? What God?

Roth deals with the issue touchingly in *The Ghost Writer*:
Nathan compares Amy Bellette's wartime travail in Europe

with his own benign experience in America:
"And what did you have instead?" she asked me.
Nathan's reply: " My childhood."
As the story ends, Amy departs, returning to her life in Cambridge. Nathan takes his leave, too, but not before watching as Lonoff's wife finally flees her unhappy marriage, on foot down the snow-covered road, with Lonoff in dogged pursuit.

Nearly 30 years after *The Ghost Writer*, Roth wrote a sequel, *Exit Ghost*, his penultimate book, the last to feature Nathan Zuckerman. It is a novel about aging, physical decline, and mortality. Nathan is now 71, living an isolated writer's life in the Berkshires, close to where E.I. Lonoff lived on that fateful day nearly 50 years earlier when Nathan first encountered him and Amy Bellette. Nathan is a refugee from New York, a recluse for the last 11 years, incontinent and impotent from prostate cancer.[27]

One day, he ventures to New York to seek treatment for his incontinence – collagen injections that he hopes will reduce the shame and embarrassment he feels. At Mount Sinai Hospital, he sees a woman who somehow reminds him of Amy Bellette. Her voice sounds familiar, and his eerie feeling is confirmed when he overhears a doctor saying her name. Now, 75, she has had surgery for brain cancer and looks alarmingly close to death. We soon learn that Amy lived with E.I. Lonoff for five years, after Hope left him. Lonoff published no more short stories, but was said to be working on a novel when he died in 1961.

Roth then develops a second story line. On a whim powered by wishful thinking about his condition, Nathan answers a newspaper ad to swap for a year his Berkshire house for a New York City apartment rented by a young married couple, Jamie Logan, a beautiful, 20-something woman from a moneyed Houston oil family, and Billy Davidoff, a nice Jewish boy who adores her. Jamie had once attended a lecture Nathan gave at Harvard. They agree to swap houses.

Nathan is immediately attracted to Jamie and has a "fantasy of regeneration." Instead of accepting his plight as "a man bearing between his legs a spigot of wrinkled flesh," he feels hope: "She had a huge pull on me, a huge gravitational pull on the ghost of my desire...I experienced the bitter helplessness of a taunted old man dying to be whole again."

Nathan imagines a sexual encounter with Jamie by scribbling a short story called "He and She." It's a parallel track to the reality unfolding, an exercise in denial by fiction.

Nathan soon receives a phone call from a former Harvard classmate of Jamie's named Richard Kliman, who was once her boyfriend. Kliman is now a 28-year-old journalist who is writing a biography about Lonoff and wants to interview Zuckerman. Nathan resists, saying there should be no biography of a long-dead writer largely forgotten, who cherished his privacy. Besides, Nathan envies Kliman's youth and vigor. He is "savage with health and armed to the teeth with time." Kliman insists Lonoff had a secret, the very same secret, rumor had it, harbored by Nathaniel Hawthorne: incest with his sister. Kliman has a copy of Lonoff's unfinished novel, given to him by Amy Bellette, and it tells of Lonoff's incest.[28]

Nathan tries to convince Kliman that Lonoff wasn't writing of his own incest with his older half-sister, but merely imagining a story derived from the rumors about Nathaniel Hawthorne. Lonoff, Nathan says, was never an autobiographical writer. His fiction "was never representation. It was rumination in narrative form." In arguing this position with Kliman, Nathan "had come to believe it myself."

Distressed by Amy's condition, frustrated by Jamie, and mad at Kliman, Nathan flees New York after only a week, returning to his Berkshires retreat, an over-the-hill man humbled by his encounters with young people trying to climb that very hill. "I passed through for the briefest moment...buffeted by the merciless encounter between the no-longers and the not-yets, only to pull out..." The novel ends starkly with Nathan Zuckerman alone again, in self-imposed exile.

Philip Roth wrote only one more book. He retired in 2013, when he turned 80, talking of the strain of writing fiction, the stamina it required. In *Exit Ghost*, Roth had confessed, via Zuckerman, his fear that he would forget "the details of the previous chapter...unable, after only a few minutes, to remember much of the previous page."

"I knew there was no sense continuing," Roth said in a later interview. "I was not going to get any better. And why get worse?" [29]

It was time to go, time to end one of the most remarkable careers in postwar literature – a Jewish writer who became an American original.

ELEVEN

Bernard Malamud: The Forgotten Man

Saul Bellow famously quipped nearly 50 years ago that he, Bernard Malamud, and Philip Roth were the Hart, Schaffner & Marx of Jewish writers. It was pointedly funny then, reflecting Bellow's irritation that he and the others were being ghettoized, like the up-scale clothier that started out in the rag trade.[1] But since Hart, Schaffner & Marx filed for bankruptcy some years back, fewer people get the joke these days. Will the time come when Bellow, Malamud and Roth are just as irrelevant?

Bellow's reputation seems secure: He will always be Nobel Laureate Saul Bellow. Roth, too, is likely to remain in the pantheon. His early books retain their following, and his later American trilogy took him to an entirely different level of accomplishment, including a Pulitzer Prize for *American Pastoral* in 1998. Malamud? I'm afraid he is becoming the forgotten man.

Once upon a time, in the 1950s and 1960s, when I first read him, Malamud could lay claim to a place in the sun. After publishing several short stories, mainly about immigrant Jews, in magazines like *Commentary* and *Partisan Review*, Malamud jumped far afield in 1952 with his first novel, *The Natural*, a baseball story about a mythic anti-hero. *The New York Times* declared it "a brilliant and unusual book," which it surely was.[2] Some 30 years later, *The Natural* was enshrined in the American vernacular when it was made into a movie starring Robert Redford.[3]

But it was the Jewish books that created his reputation. *The Assistant*, published in 1957, is widely regarded as his best novel, a homespun parable about Morris Bober, a wretchedly poor grocer in Brooklyn, and his relationship with his Gentile assistant, Frank Alpine. Philip Roth, in eulogizing Malamud in 1986, called *The Assistant* a "masterpiece,"[4] and *Time* magazine, as recently as 2010, listed it as one of the 100 best books published in English,[5] right up there with Bellow's *Augie March* and *Herzog*, as well as Roth's *Portnoy's Complaint* and *American Pastoral*. A year after *The Assistant*, Malamud published *The Magic Barrel*, a collection of short stories that won the National Book Award, besting Vladimir Nabokov's *Lolita*. It was one of the few times a collection of short stories won the award — a tribute, I think, to Malamud's use of folklore, myth, and magical realism in his tales of immigrant Jews.

Finally, in 1966, Malamud hit the jackpot with his fourth novel, *The Fixer*, which managed the rare feat of winning both the National Book Award and the Pulitzer Prize for fiction — this for a bleak book set in Czarist Russia that tells the story of a poor Jew, Yakov Bok, falsely imprisoned for the ritual murder of a Russian boy. Critics often used the same words to describe Malamud's work during this period: He wrote parables, compassionate and wise, about ordinary and moral people who were struggling to find meaning and redemption amid their bleak circumstances.

But Malamud's other novels, less about Jewish themes, generally received poor or mixed reviews, much to my surprise and dismay. Bellow, of all people, damned *A New Life* as "dead... mean and humorless." In a private letter to Harvey Swados, Bellow said that when Malamud "enlarges his scope, or tries to, he comes up with all the middle-class platitudes of love and liberalism." [6] In other words, Brother Malamud, stick to what you know best: the suffering of all those Jews who show their moral courage in coping with a hostile world.

Malamud suffered a stroke in 1982 that ended his writing career at age 67, and he died four years later. Over the next 25 years, his work gradually fell out of favor, even as Bellow and Roth gained preeminence. Bellow's view of Malamud became conventional wisdom. Malamud's obituary in the *New York Times*, for example, cited "a growing bleakness in his work," adding that "as he left his Jewish milieu for ... other settings, his work took on a flinty emptiness without the poignance and meaning" of his earlier fiction. [7] Even Malamud's daughter conceded his fall from literary grace: "What was once a trio of Bellow, Malamud, and Roth became a dyad," Janna Malamud Smith wrote in her touching and honest 2006 memoir, *My Father is a Book*. [8]

His friends, supported by some critics, have fought to

preserve Malamud's reputation as one of the best writers of his generation. His family, abandoning its quest for privacy, agreed to provide material for a biography written by Philip Davis, a British academic, who admitted that his goal was to "seek more recognition and more readers for Malamud in the future." Fortunately, his 2007 book made the case while remaining fair-minded, scholarly, and insightful.[9]

In 2014, on the 100th anniversary of Malamud's birth, the Library of America bestowed its prestige on Malamud by publishing all his work in three volumes, a rare honor. Cynthia Ozick, favorably reviewing the new edition on the front page of the *New York Times Book Review*, paid tribute to Malamud's entire oeuvre, lamenting his declining place in American literature. "A new generation, mostly unacquainted with the risks of uncompromising and hard-edged compassion, deserves Malamud even more" than his own contemporary readership once did.[10]

The drive to restore Malamud's popularity or reputation hasn't much changed things, I'm sorry to say. When he is remembered at all, it is for his short stories and for his one undeniably brilliant novel, *The Assistant*. The movie version of *The Natural* is recalled once in a while, but this is small consolation since it so radically changed the book's ending and corrupted its meaning. In *Exit Ghost*, published in 2007, Roth has Nathan Zuckerman say of E.I. Lonoff, who is modeled after Malamud: "Nobody reads him. Nobody remembers him."

Is the judgment of history fair? Or should we reassess Malamud?

Because many years had passed since I originally read

most of Malamud's fiction, I decided to take another look — to see whether I thought Malamud's work stood the test of time. And I wanted to understand more of Malamud's take on Jewish identity, which turned out to have some surprising twists. As part of the exercise, I also read much more about Malamud's life, which is important, as Davis says, "because of the tense closeness of the life and the work, and the struggle between them." Malamud, he says, made "imagination out of memory." [11]

The memories were harsh. His father, Max, an immigrant from Russia, ran a small grocery store in Brooklyn. For many years the family lived over the store, and Malamud was ashamed of his family's dire poverty — and the mental illness that plagued his mother and his younger brother, Eugene.

When he was 13, Malamud returned home from school one day to find his mother lying on the kitchen floor, frothing at the mouth. There was an empty can of disinfectant ("something like Drano") in one hand. "He ran to the neighborhood drugstore for aid — a powder, a medicine — that he and the druggist spooned into her," wrote Smith in her memoir of her father. [12] He had saved his mother's life. She was hospitalized and never returned home. She died in a mental hospital two years later, possibly a suicide, a victim of schizophrenia. (Eugene was also a schizophrenic, in and out of mental institutions, supported emotionally and financially by Malamud.)

"The moment in the kitchen exploded through him," Smith wrote, "an immeasurable betrayal...It damaged his natural being, his ability to live easily, openly, casually in the everyday world. His trust."

A strong public education saved him, first at P.S. 181 and Erasmus Hall High School, both in Brooklyn, then at tuition-free City College of New York. At CCNY, he was tutored in writing by Teddy Goodman, a charismatic teacher who remained a friend until his death in 1952, just after Malamud published his first novel, *The Natural*. (One of Malamud's classmates at City College was Alfred Kazin, who became a noted literary critic and admirer of Malamud's work.) After graduating in 1936 during the depth of the Depression, Malamud supported himself largely by teaching in high schools in Brooklyn, earning a master's degree along the way from Columbia, where he wrote a dissertation on Thomas Hardy.

Malamud always understood the role his early memories played throughout his lifetime. "People say I write so much about misery," he once said... "but you cannot obliterate your earlier experience...it stays with you." [13]

And so it did, providing real-life grist for his literary mill, infusing him with remarkable determination to succeed as a writer, and shaping his lapidary work habits. "He continued to feel deeply oppressed by the narrowness of [his father's] existence," his daughter wrote..."He felt terrified about somehow losing...the lone exit visa he possessed from that fate: his hope of becoming a major writer."

Just before his marriage to Ann deChiara in 1945, Malamud made it clear to his wife-to-be that his writing would always come first: "I must repeat again what marriage to me will mean for you. Though I love you and shall love you more, most of my strength will be devoted to realizing myself as an artist." [14]

Like clockwork, except on days when he was teaching, Malamud took himself to his writing room every morning right after breakfast and brooked no interruption. In the evenings, he devoted himself to reading. He carried a small notebook with him at all times, often jotting down words and ideas. He always seemed preoccupied, lost in thought, rewriting in his head. He wrote in blue or black ink on yellow unlined paper, with plenty of space for revisions. He began each day by reading and rewriting what he had written the day before. Ann would type and retype the drafts – usually two or three times, occasionally ten times or more. On a good day, Malamud managed to coax out of himself half a page of finished copy, those plain words and simple stories that he used so effectively to probe moral complexity. "He understood that effort and discipline made up his strong suit," his daughter wrote.

Sometimes, his sentences carried the cadence of Yiddish, and his dialogue was often a blend that Malamud called "Yinglish." ("You should sell long ago the store," said Morris's wife, Ida, in *The Assistant*.) Philip Roth described it this way: "Malamud wrote of a meager world of pain in a language all his own... the locutions, inversions, and diction of Jewish immigrant speech, a heap of broken verbal bones...that he made dance to his sad tune." [15]

Malamud sometimes joked about his work habits. In later life, he often told the story that Roth had told him: When Roth, hardly a slacker, occasionally found it hard to get started in the morning, he would goad himself to work by saying to himself: "Malamud has already been working for three hours." [16]

Once, when Malamud was seeking a college teaching job, Ann typed and mailed 200 letters to colleges that might hire someone who lacked a PhD. Oregon State College, an agricultural school that specialized in animal husbandry, agreed to let Malamud teach English composition, but not literature. Malamud, Ann, and their son, Paul, moved to Corvallis, Oregon in 1949.

In 1952, Malamud received a telegram in Corvallis from Robert Giroux, who was to become his lifelong editor and friend, saying that Harcourt Brace had agreed to publish his first novel, *The Natural*.[17] Malamud was 38. A baseball novel without one Jewish character, *The Natural* seems far afield from the concerns Malamud had shown in his earlier short stories about immigrant Jews, a literary reach for a bookish Jew who "threw a baseball like a girl," as one of his friends once put it.[18]

When I first read *The Natural* as a teenager, soon after it was published, it was a baseball story, plain and simple. All the iconic baseball legends were there in barely disguised form: Babe Ruth promising sick kids in the hospital that he would hit a home run for them. Shoeless Joe Jackson throwing baseball games to win his gambling bets. Even the incident that precipitated the book: Eddie Waitkus of the Philadelphia Phillies getting shot by a woman fan.

Little did I know until later – much later – that Malamud was pursuing the themes that marked all his fiction, especially the struggle for redemption. Nor did I realize that there was a larger mythology at work here. No mere baseball story, critics pointed out, this was a tale of bigger legends, of Sir Percival and his quest for the Holy Grail, of his visit to King Arthur's Camelot, and of his quest to be a knight.

Roy Hobbs, the natural, was a brilliant creation: a superstar who was an anti-hero, and Malamud uses the techniques of magical realism so evident in his short stories. We first meet Roy as a talented 19-year-old pitcher seeking to be the best ever. But he is instead shot in a hotel room by a deranged woman who stalks fame-seeking athletes. Roy disappears for 15 years, returning as a Babe Ruth figure, a slugger for the New York Knights, who carries around his own magical bat, "Wonderboy."

Like the Babe, Roy has a gargantuan appetite for hot dogs and fast women. But he lusts after the wrong gal – a gold-digging moll named Memo Paris, who hangs around with gamblers – while rejecting Iris Lemon, the far better choice. To win Memo's love by getting rich, he agrees to take a $35,000 bribe to throw the crucial game when the Knights are on the verge of winning the pennant. Each time he comes to the plate, though troubled by what he is doing, he deliberately blows his chance.

Toward the end of the game, he realizes his love for Iris, now pregnant with his child, and vows to atone for the error of his ways. In his last at-bat, with the game on the line, he tries to hit a home run. Here, Malamud turns baseball heroics upside down: Like mighty Casey, Roy strikes out. There is no joy in Mudville, no redemption in New York. When the game is over, a little boy comes up to Roy: "Say it ain't true, Roy." Instead, Malamud writes, "he wept many bitter tears."

Though not a "Jewish" book, *The Natural* contains many of the Malamud themes so evident in his later novels: the struggle to overcome suffering, the quest for meaning, the dream of a new life. Roy loses his chance for baseball immortality, and he wins a measure of personal redemption only when he finally understands the difference between his self-centered existence and the possibility of a larger purpose in life.

In the movie version of *The Natural*, released more than 30 years later, the ending is radically changed. Roy hits a home run, and the Knights win the pennant. Even though the novel's meaning is corrupted, Malamud didn't seem to mind, taking pleasure that the public was now more likely to think of him not as a Jewish writer but as an American writer.[19]

There's no fantasy or magical realism in Malamud's next novel, *The Assistant*. It is thoroughly naturalistic in its gritty, feel-the-poverty depictions of his characters. It is also decidedly spiritual, invoking Judeo-Christian morality in surprising ways. And it is partly an autobiographical book, set in the grim grocery store of Malamud's Brooklyn youth.

The grocer, Morris Bober, opens his store every morning at six, dutifully making sure he's there to provide a Polish woman with a roll for three cents, and hauling in the waiting crates of milk. One morning, he is robbed by two masked men, who hit him over the head. A few days later, a stranger named Frank Alpine appears and offers to work for no wages in Morris's grocery in order, he says, to gain experience as a shopkeeper. It doesn't take long to realize that, unbeknownst to Morris, Frank was one of the robbers. He volunteers to help Morris as a form of atonement, and Morris, recovering from his head injury, reluctantly agrees to let Frank be his assistant.

Frank tries to right himself from his troubled life, but can't shed his bad ways. Though he manages to build the business a bit, he steals from the cash register and spies on Helen, Morris's 23-year-old daughter, when she's taking a shower. Through many twists and turns, Frank and Helen eventually grow close, furtively meeting in a nearby library or park and sharing kisses. Helen tells Frank of her dream of saving enough money from her job as a secretary to go to college. She plays Pygmalion, urging the uneducated Frank to read *Anna Karenina, Crime and Punishment*, and other great books, which she gives him from the library. Against all odds, Helen falls for him, and Frank's lust turns to love.

Meantime, an odd father-son relationship develops between Morris and Frank, the Jew and the Gentile, much of it centered on discussions of religion. Frank invokes Saint Francis of Assisi from his Catholic orphanage days and asks Morris questions about being Jewish. How is it, he wants to know, that Morris eats ham and otherwise doesn't appear to follow Jewish ritual? And why does he seem to accept the suffering of his meager life with so little complaint?

"This is not important to me if I taste pig or if I don't," Morris tells Frank. "Nobody will tell me that I am not Jewish because I put in my mouth once in a while...a piece ham. But they will tell me, and I will believe them, if I forget the Law. This means to do what is right, to be honest, to be good... to other people...This is what a Jew believes."

"I think other religions have those ideas too," Frank replies. "But tell me why it is that Jews suffer so damn much, Morris? It seems to me they like to suffer, don't they?"

"If you live, you suffer," Morris says. "I think if a Jew don't suffer for the Law, he will suffer for nothing."

"What do you suffer for," Morris?

"I suffer for you," Morris answers.

There it is: In this revealing dialogue, Malamud equates suffering with Judaism and anoints Morris as a kind of Jesus figure. "Jews in Malamud's world are the true Christians," says, Jonathan Rosen, in his introduction to the widely read paperback edition of *The Assistant*.[20] As he and others see it, *The Assistant* follows a classic Christian narrative: a man suffers, is transformed by his suffering, and finds salvation.

The novel has its own stunning conclusion. Frank's original partner in crime against Morris, Ward Minogue, attempts to rape Helen. Frank thwarts the rape, only to succumb to his own lust for Helen by forcing himself on her. "Dog," she cries. "Uncircumcised dog."

Some time later, after Morris has died from pneumonia, Frank dons Morris's apron and assumes his role behind the counter of the shabby grocery store. "One day in April," Malamud writes in the novel's last few lines, "Frank went to the hospital and had himself circumcised. For a couple of days he dragged himself around with a pain between his legs. The pain enraged and inspired him. After Passover he became a Jew."

Malamud's vision of Morris as saintly Jew reverberated for years. In a 1974 essay, Philip Roth took on Malamud, his friend and literary father-figure, criticizing the very novels he professed to admire, *The Assistant* and *The Fixer*. In a complicated argument, Roth faulted Malamud for creating Jewish characters who were suffering Jews, virtuous victims, full of passive "righteousness and restraint," and lacking any "libidinous or aggressive activities." [21] Though he didn't use the phrase, Roth painted them as Christ-like in their poverty, pain, moral goodness, and quest for redemption. By contrast, the Christian characters, especially Frank Alpine, were full of sexual lust and transgressive behavior – the bad *goy* to Morris Bober's saintly Jew. *The Assistant*, Roth wrote, was a book of "stern morality" – the same book he later called a "masterpiece."

Roth contrasted Malamud's protagonists to the exuberant Jewish characters created by Saul Bellow, especially the picaresque Augie March, and his own hypersexual Alexander Portnoy. He even invoked Norman Mailer's provocative essay, "The White Negro," published the same year as *The Assistant*, in which Mailer found much to praise in characters who were bold, hyper-sexual and aggressive to the point of transgression. In effect, according to Roth, Malamud had created Jewish protagonists who were stereotypes, not fully realized human beings.

Malamud, often lauded for his humanity, was stunned. He drafted two letters to Roth, accusing him of misrepresentation and refuting his arguments. He never sent them. Instead, Malamud mailed only a few words from the conclusion of his draft: "It's your problem."

In an essay published just after Malamud died...Roth says he wrote back to Malamud, audaciously insisting that he had done him a favor by pointing out "fictional skeletons" that perhaps Malamud himself didn't realize.[22] Little wonder that Malamud had declined to talk to Roth for several years. They were reconciled in May 1978 when Malamud and his wife, Ann, accepted a dinner invitation in London from Roth and Claire Bloom, who were then living together. The two men kissed on the lips and resumed their friendship.[23]

However, in a letter to his daughter in May 1978, a week

after the dinner of reconciliation, Malamud did voice his true feelings: Roth, he said, had written a "foolish egoistic essay about my work" and had "certainly misinterpreted" *The Assistant*. The letter was not made public until 2006, some 20 years after Malamud had died.[24]

Yet Roth and others were not alone in their criticism. The charge that *The Assistant* was a "Christian" book was repeated in 2000 in *The Modern Jewish Canon* by Harvard professor Ruth Wisse, who dismissed Malamud as a Jewish writer. Why? Because he "identifies the Jew exclusively and ideologically with the archetype of the sufferer, and on this basis imagines the Jew as the ideal Christian...The Judaism to which Alpine converts is really a purer ethical form of his own Catholicism."[25]

Wisse had a similar complaint about *The Fixer*, a novel set in Czarist Russia. The protagonist, a non-religious Jew named Yakov Bok, is imprisoned on the false charge that he murdered a Russian boy to use his blood in the baking of Passover matzos —a common anti-Semitic slur at the time. Malamud writes of Yakov's suffering in prison, his yearning for freedom, and his refusal to confess to a crime he didn't commit. Malamud's story was based on the real-life trial of Mendel Beilis, who in 1911 was charged with the same crime of ritual murder. As Wisse sees it, Malamud converts Beilus, a "simple Jew," into "a quasi-intellectual free-thinker...universalizing his plight and distancing him from Jewish religion."[26]

Thus, with incredible irony and questionable reasoning, Malamud's work was considered not Jewish enough to be included in the Jewish canon by one of America's leading scholars of Jewish literature. Malamud, like Bellow and Roth, didn't want to be defined as a "Jewish writer," but Wisse had excommunicated him from the literary tribe. Am I the only one who thinks this absurd?

At the same time, many other critics were faulting Malamud for the very opposite sin: straying far beyond his natural milieu of the suffering Jew seeking redemption. In 1961, Malamud published *A New Life*, which he saw as "an American novel... different from anything I've ever done." [27] It told the story of S. Levin, a New Yorker and former alcoholic, who seeks to rebuild his life in the greener pastures of the Pacific Northwest, where he goes to teach at the fictional Cascadia College. Though the novel has many retrospective defenders, including Morris Dickstein[28] and Cynthia Ozick[29], other critics found Malamud way out of his comfort zone. Even Saul Bellow thought Malamud should stick to his *Yiddishkeit* knitting.[30] Malamud was thus damned if he did, and damned if he didn't.

As the conventional 1950s morphed into the radical 1960s, Malamud seemed like a man left behind, a writer whose time and place had passed. An era of protest and counter-culture had little use for Malamud's verities of suffering, stoicism, and endurance. His editor, Robert Giroux, described it as a "starvation period – a spare period when the juices weren't working." [31]

Malamud did try to branch out. After *The Fixer* was published in 1966, and won both the National Book Award and the Pulitzer Prize, Malamud wrote *The Tenants* in 1971, about two writers, one black, one Jewish, living in a tenement. It was Malamud's attempt to explore racial issues, as well as a meditation on writing, but it received lukewarm reviews.

Malamud fared better with *Dubin's Lives*, published in 1979, which Malamud intended as his "big book," [32] the anguished tale of William Dubin, a 56-year old biographer, juggling a career, wife, children, and a mistress. Dubin is Malamud's most autobiographical character, and Malamud once told his friend, Bert Pogrebin, that if "you know *Dubin's Lives*, you know me." Bert repeated the story to the guys in our book group during our discussion of the book.[33] Much of Malamud's life is here – Dubin as a boy saving his mother from suicide on the kitchen floor, and Dubin in middle age taking on a college-age mistress, as Malamud did when he was teaching at Bennington College. The book got mostly strong reviews, and I very much liked it, but the book didn't live up to Malamud's hopes for it, or his publisher's great expectations.

In 1982, Malamud went far afield with *God's Grace*, which took on the theme of nuclear annihilation. Calvin Cohn, the sole survivor of a nuclear war, finds himself on an island with chimpanzees and apes, and tries to re-start evolution. Here, Malamud takes magical realism to a new level, including a Passover seder of talking chimpanzees. It all seemed preposterous to me, and the critics generally dismissed *God's Grace* as a book whose cosmic reach far exceeded Malamud's mundane grasp.

In 1982, just after *God's Grace* was published, Malamud suffered a stroke while undergoing heart surgery. He was never the same. He had difficulty recalling words and couldn't write with anything like his former style. "All that he had held at bay since boyhood seemed to collapse in upon him," said his daughter. "He became to himself a diminished, frail, uncertain man." [34] He died four years later, at 71.

For all his success, Malamud never felt that he had escaped the shadow of Saul Bellow, his contemporary, friend, and rival. When Bellow won the Nobel Prize in 1976, Malamud wrote in his notebook: "October 21. Bellow gets Nobel Prize. I win $24.25 in poker."[35] His friend, Letty Cottin Pogrebin, thought Malamud saw himself as Salieri to Bellow's Mozart – never the genius, always the runner-up.[36] Malamud himself thought Bellow's prose was richer than his own. "He uses two words to my one," he once said.[37] But Malamud's style was elegant in its own distilled way, the product of all that re-writing. Perhaps he envied Bellow's felicity, the ease with which the words seemed to pour out. Nothing ever came easy for Malamud.

Bellow outlived Malamud by 19 years, remaining in the public eye as literary eminence and bon vivant. In their contrasting lifestyles, said Malamud's publisher, Roger Straus, "Saul Bellow was filet mignon, Malamud was hamburger."[38] Roth, too, remained a literary force well into his 80s, his provocative life often an open book.

Because Malamud's name was usually linked to Bellow's and Roth's, it was perhaps inevitable he would suffer by comparison, eclipsed by their formidable output and enhanced reputations. For those who care, Malamud will be remembered for the brilliance of his short stories ("Four or five of the best American short stories I'd ever read," said Roth[39]), for his one undeniably great book, *The Assistant*, and for at least three others that more than passed literary muster (*The Natural, A New Life* and *Dubin's Lives*).

If, by some stroke of magical realism, no one had ever heard of Bellow or Roth, perhaps Malamud would have escaped his fate as the forgotten man of a golden age. He certainly deserves better.

TWELVE

Greenhorns and Yankees

When Bernard Malamud's first novel, *The Natural*, was published in 1952, I was 13, the very pinnacle of my baseball obsession. Specifically, I was a Yankees fan. So the saga of superstar Roy Hobbs fit right into the lore of Babe Ruth, Lou Gehrig, Joe DiMaggio, Mickey Mantle, and the other Bronx Bombers. When I re-read the book recently, I got to thinking about why the New York Yankees took hold of Jewish kids like me in the Bronx.

The Yankees were the Establishment, after all, the elitist Upper Class of America's National Pastime, while the Bronx had long been the opposite: Home of the immigrants, the working class, the underdogs, the ethnic minorities, the Jews. But far from rejecting this foreign object in our midst, as if it were an organ transplant, we very much embraced the Yankees.

And why not? Yes, success often breeds resentment, and

there have always been Yankee-haters abroad in the land. But if you were born and bred in the Bronx, then the most Jewish of New York's five boroughs, what could be more American, more emblematic of making it, than the New York Yankees? We knew in our collective gut that the Yankees were the inspiration for our own lives. Goodbye, Greenhorn. I'm a Yankee Doodle Dandy.

But if we were thrilled by the Yankees' success, how do we explain why the kids from Brooklyn, not much different from us in their ethnicity, their Jewishness, and their striving, were attracted to the Dodgers, those perennial losers? And lose they did – some five times to the Yankees in the World Series in 1941, 1947, 1949, 1952, and 1953. The Brooklyn Bums even managed to blow a 13-game lead in the National League pennant race in 1951, culminating in the legendary play-off game against the New York Giants, when Bobby Thompson hit a ninth-inning home run off Ralph Branca in the old Polo Grounds, the Giants home field in Upper Manhattan. It remains one of the most stunning moments in baseball history, the very symbol of epic collapse.

Nonetheless, Brooklyn fans retained their love for the Dodgers, as if they had taken a marriage vow to remain faithful for better or worse, till death do us part. I suppose the Dodgers represented another side of ethnic New York, another version of the immigrant experience – this one an identification with the underdogs of society, especially after Jackie Robinson joined the Dodgers in 1947 as the first black player in the major leagues. Perhaps, too, they harbored the immigrant hope for a better future. "Wait till next year," was their rallying cry after every failure to win the pennant or World Series loss.

"Next year" finally came in 1955, when the Brooklyn Bums did beat the Bronx Bombers in a World Series. But they soon broke Brooklyn's heart by bolting for the lucrative field of dreams in Los Angeles. As part of the deal, the Giants fled New York, too, setting up camp in San Francisco. Both Ebbetts Field in Brooklyn and the Polo Grounds in Manhattan were soon torn down, replaced by bleak public housing, leaving not a trace of their colorful past.

The villain of the piece was Walter O'Malley, the Dodgers' owner, who orchestrated the transcontinental shift. O'Malley could claim – and he did – that in opening up the West he had made baseball a truly national pastime. But he was so reviled in Brooklyn that he needed a bodyguard. One joke making the rounds: "If you had a gun with only two bullets in it and were in a room with Hitler, Stalin, and O'Malley, who would you shoot? Answer: O'Malley, twice!" [1]

The Yankees moved, too, but only across the street to a new stadium opened in 2009. In a nod to us old-timers, the new ballpark has visual echoes of the old place, and you can still see the Jerome Avenue el train passing just beyond the right-center field bleachers, just as it always did. Except today it's called the Number 4 train.

Knowing of my Yankee fandom, my daughter, Sarah, suggested we hold my 70th birthday party at the newly opened Yankee Stadium – a kind of going back to my roots. After a certain age, birthdays tend toward nostalgic indulgence, and so it was for my 70th. Along with the hot dogs and beer, there was plenty of sacred talk about stickball games, egg creams, and seltzer bottles, as if they were artifacts of an ancient civilization. But I have to confess that we rented a private suite for the occasion, which was a rather egregious upgrade from the bleachers of my youth.

Reflecting on the past, I found myself thinking about the Brooklyn Dodgers as well as the Yankees. They were two sides of the same immigrant coin. If Yankee fans of yore wanted to identify with success, Dodger fans took comfort in longing for better days ahead. We each played the hand we were dealt. It just worked out a bit better for those of us from the Bronx.

THIRTEEN

The Jewish John Updike

Just as there are many ways to be Jewish, there are many ways Jewish-American writers have expressed their Jewishness. Or not. Malamud was perhaps the most traditionally Jewish, often writing with great humanity of the immigrant experience. Bellow created many memorable Jewish characters, but strived to be American. Roth was funny and biting in his satire of Jewish life. And Salinger or Mailer? Well, you wouldn't know they were Jewish from most of their writing.

Then there's John Updike. Yes, *that* John Updike – the highly prolific Protestant, the master of all literary forms, perhaps the greatest stylist of his generation. A big fan, I read just about everything he wrote, when he wrote it. Updike is best known for his middle-American "Rabbit" novels and his exquisite short stories of suburban life and love. Along the way, he turned out essays, book reviews, and a single piece of sports writing that ranks with the best, "Hub Fans Bid Kid Adieu,"

about Ted Williams' last game at Fenway Park. [1] Oh, yes, Updike also wrote three books of satirical fiction about a Jewish novelist named Henry Bech. They are Updike's "Jewish"
books, and they raise a lot of questions about Jewish identity
and what constitutes Jewish-American literature.

The character of Henry Bech was born in a short story,
"The Bulgarian Poetess," that ran in *The New Yorker* in March
1965. [2] It was based on Updike's own travels in Eastern Europe,
as an emissary for the State Department, and very much reflected the conflict he felt between being a private writer and a
public man. Bech retraces Updike's path, but in different ways
and for different reasons. A bachelor in his 40s, Bech had written a highly successful first novel, *Travelling Light*, that had
echoes of Jack Kerouac. He wrote three more books that fell
flat, one of them badly roughed up by the critics.

Bech then descended into a colossal writer's block reminiscent of Henry Roth or J.D. Salinger. ("Am I blocked?" Bech
asks. "I just thought of myself as a slow typist.") The drought
is so bad that Bech receives the Melville Medal, "awarded every five years to that American author who has maintained the
most meaningful silence." Unable to write, Bech chooses to
become a celebrity, knowing full well that he is trying to escape the burden of being a writer, veering "between the harlot-
ry of the lecture platform and the torture of the writing desk."

Partly because most of the major American writers at the
time were Jewish, Updike made Henry Bech a Jew – non-obser-
vant, but clearly Jewish with "thin curling hair and melancholy
Jewish nose." In the very-obvious heyday of Jewish-American
writers, Updike said, "a Jewish writer is almost as inevitable as

an Italian gangster." [3] But to Updike, Bech was more clearly a writer, "a literary man," than he was a Jew.

The Bech character might have disappeared after one appearance, but "The Bulgarian Poetess" won the O. Henry Award in 1966 for best short story, and Updike soon wrote several more Bech stories, gathering them in *Bech: A Book*, published in 1970. Two more books followed: *Bech is Back* (1982) and *Bech at Bay* (1998). The three books contain 20 stories, and Updike regarded them as collections of short stories, not novels.[4] The Bech books do lack some of the dramatic buildup of a novel, but they achieve narrative flow and continuity via the comic character of Henry Bech. Much to Updike's surprise, *Bech: A Book* was widely praised upon publication in 1970, cited by some reviewers as Updike's best book. He said, not entirely in jest, to Judith Jones, his editor at Knopf: "Somehow, as everyone treats Bech so courteously, I'm beginning to wonder if there isn't a Jewish Mafia." [5]

The Bech character, modeled partly after Bellow, Malamud, Roth, and Mailer, enabled Updike to comment on the writer's life in mid-century America. It was, Updike has said, " a way of unpacking the kinds of experience that only a writer has...via an alter ego who wasn't myself...It permits me to write without holding back." [6] And it allowed Updike, normally a critic of great decorum, to settle some scores while parodying other writers and critics with satiric abandon. "I made Bech as unlike myself as I could," Updike has said. "Instead of being married with four children, he is a bachelor; instead of being a gentile, he's a Jew." [7] And instead of a boyhood in rural Pennsylvania and an adult life in small-town Massachusetts, Bech is a denizen of Manhattan's Upper West Side, born and bred. And where Updike is prolific, Bech is blocked. But Bech does share some characteristics with Updike. Both are filled with existential dread ("a fleck of dust condemned to know it is a fleck of dust," Bech fears). Both hope writing books will confer a degree of immortality. Both dwell on sex ("that hint of eternal life"), and Updike gleefully enables Bech to bed nearly every woman in sight, except the one who got away, the blond and beautiful Vera Glavanakova, the Bulgarian poetess in the first Bech story.

A dozen years later, in 1982, Updike published the second Bech book, about the same time as his third Rabbit novel. The fun continued. After more travels abroad, Bech, still blocked, supports himself by speaking at colleges. "There, he was hauled from the creative-writing class to the faculty cocktail party to the John D. Benefactor Memorial Auditorium and thence, baffled applause still ringing in his ears, back to the Holiday Inn."

Bech marries Bea, sister of his former mistress, and moves to her suburban house with her three children in Ossining, New York, famous for John Cheever and Sing Sing prison. We are here treated to all the old Updike magic when he writes about couples in suburbia – the details of wife-wooing, of married sex, of adultery, all limned in that majestic style. Only this time, there is more of the writer's life – the struggle to produce a novel, the spousal support to overcome writer's block, and finally the ultimate reward of a best-seller with the portentous title of *Thinking Big*. Though panned by critics, this is the long-awaited novel, 15 years in the making, that told us that Bech is back.

Here in the Christian redoubt of his wife's ancestral home, Bech's, Jewishness rears its head, mostly in response to Bea's criticisms of the characters in *Thinking Big*.

"Do you realize," Bea stings, "there isn't a Gentile character in here who isn't in love with some Jew?" As Bea sees it, the Gentile characters are treated as "hooligans...a barbaric people." She suggests a new title for his book: "Jews vs. Jerks." It doesn't take long for the marriage to fail, and for Bech to move back to his homeland on the Upper West Side.

With the success of *Thinking Big*, Bech makes the most of his new celebrity. He becomes president of a salon called "The Forty," an elitist academy of artists, writers, and musicians dedicated to their own aggrandizement. Bech loves the prestige of it, the authority that comes with his tenure as president. And, always priapic, he uses his position to seduce women. It is Updike's way of spoofing the arts establishment, those pretentious swells who defend the status quo against anything the least bit innovative that might threaten their standing.

Over the years, Updike broadened the satire in the Bech books. By the third iteration, published nearly 30 years after the first, Updike has Bech taking on the critics. This is clearly pay back time for Updike, who took his share of hits, especially in the early years. Critics complained that while Updike wrote like an angel he had nothing much to say – "a minor novelist with a major style," in the words of Harold Bloom.[8] There's nothing subtle about Bech's revenge against his own fictitious critics: In a chapter called "Bech Noir," he simply kills off three of them by ingenious means impossible to detect.

He's aided in the last murder by his latest girlfriend, Rachel Teagarten, known as Robin, who proves to be a faithful sidekick to the Bechman. She's 26 to Beck's 75 and "post-Jewish." She insists on having Bech's child, and if he balks, she threatens to blackmail him by revealing the murders. So at 76, Bech becomes a father for the first time, to a daughter who is given the not-very "post-Jewish" name of Golda.

In the last Bech story, Updike sticks it to the Swedes who repeatedly grant the Nobel Prize to obscure foreign writers (Dario Fo, anyone?) rather than major Americans like Philip Roth, Thomas Pynchon, or Updike himself. Yes, Henry Bech, blocked writer with a meager output, wins the Nobel Prize for Literature.

The news is greeted with delicious outrage. *The New York Times* calls Bech "a passé exponent of fancy penmanship." *New York* magazine has John Simon, that grand curmudgeon, write a retrospective entitled, "The Case (Farfetched) for Henry Bech." And the *New York Daily News* simply headlines, "BECH? WHO DAT?"

Bech journeys to Sweden, agonizing over his acceptance speech. He ascends the podium, rapt dignitaries in attendance, with 10-month-old Golda in his arms. Sure enough, after some words of writerly wisdom, he develops speaker's block: He has nothing else to say. As if on cue, Golda, comes to the rescue. She says "hi" to the grandees in the room, "pronounced with a bright distinctness instantly amplified into the depths of the beautiful, infinite hall. Then she lifted her right hand, where all could see, and made the gentle clasping and unclasping motion that signifies bye-bye."

By making Bech Jewish, Updike had more in mind than simply reflecting the heyday of the Jewish-American writers who were his contemporaries. It's no secret that many of his harshest critics were Jews. Norman Podhoretz, the editor of *Commentary*, was a constant scourge. Updike's short stories, Podhoretz wrote, "strike me as all windup and no delivery," and his prose was "bloated like a child who had eaten too much candy." [9] And Leslie Fiedler once called Updike, "a strangely irrelevant writer." [10]

Updike uses Bech to fight some of his battles, especially against Podhoretz. In an interview, Updike said, "I try not," in my head, "to satisfy reviewers or to placate Norman Podhoretz...or any of the other people who have been really out to puncture me. I think they can't be placated..." [11]

But they can be parodied. Henry Bech becomes a major contributor to *Commentary*, much celebrated in its pages. Much of the humor is aimed squarely at Podhoretz, and Updike is upfront about it: "I've never been warmly treated by the *Commentary* crowd – insofar as it is a crowd – and so I made Bech its darling. Norman Podhoretz has always gone out of his way to slam me, and this was my way of having some fun with him," he said in a 1973 interview with Frank Gaddo. [12]

Updike even created a five-page, fake bibliography for the fictitious Bech, including titles of bogus essays in very real magazines (including *Commentary*, *The New Republic*, and *Partisan Review*) by such critics as Fiedler and Alfred Kazin. Updike is clearly having fun with his inside joke, producing wonderful parody.

In an interview for a *Time* magazine cover story in 1982,

Updike went even further: "...I created Henry Bech to show that I was really a Jewish writer also." [13] Updike was teasing, but presumably he wanted to demonstrate a broader range, as he did in other books over the years.

Updike was hardly the first Christian writer to create a Jewish character. There was, of course, Shakespeare's Shylock, Dickens' Fagin, and Hemingway's Robert Cohn in *The Sun Also Rises* – all stereotypes beyond the point of anti-Semitism. And Jewish writers were not shy about creating Gentile characters, from Bellow's Henderson to Salinger's Holden Caulfield. Mark Twain went even further, speaking in the voice of Jim, the runaway slave who floats down the Mississippi in *Huckleberry Finn*. In short, writers have always been free to create fictional characters far from their family tree.

Yet some Jewish writers were offended by the Bech improvisation, as if Updike had trespassed on their turf, like an illegal immigrant who had to be stopped at the border. When the first Bech book was published, Cynthia Ozick, leveled a blistering attack on Updike for creating an inauthentic Jew, a character whose Jewishness is only skin deep, and thus somehow demeaning to honest-to-God Jewish literature. As a Jew, Ozick writes, Bech "is an imbecile to the core..." He's "a switch on a literary computer...cranked on whenever Updike reminds himself that he is obliged to produce a sociological symptom: crank, gnash: and out flies an inverted sentence." [14]

For Ozick, Bech isn't Jewish enough, lacking the sort of religious feeling Updike frequently attributes to his Christian characters. "In the case of Bech – and *only* in the case of Bech – Updike does not find it worthwhile to be theological," Ozick wrote. "He is the only major character in Updike's fiction wholly untouched by the transcendental." [15] Fair point, but why does that make the Bech character any less Jewish than, say, Norman Mailer?

By the time the second Bech book came out, Ozick allowed that it was "greatly refined" in tone, but that "Bech is no more a Jewish character than I am a WASP." And by the third book, Ozick conceded that Bech is becoming more Jewish, reading the Bible, taking Hebrew lessons. "Bech, as Jew, is like a little child, though pushing 60."

I have no quarrel if Ozick doesn't find Bech a convincing protagonist. But she defines Jewishness as requiring a religious test. "To be a Jew is to be covenanted," she writes, defining Jews as Biblical people who made a covenant with God – people chosen to show the world a monotheist God in return for a promised land. In other words, no secular Jew need apply. Says Updike scholar Sanford Pinsker: "Granted, Bech is neither more – nor less – than a literary Jew, and if this means he is not a member in good standing of Ozick's synagogue, so be it." [16]

Even if we accept Updike's Bech into the tribe, over Ozick's fierce objection, do the Bech books, in some sense, belong in the tradition of Jewish-American fiction? Can a Christian, in other words, write a "Jewish book?"

Some of the themes expressed via Bech, says Updike scholar Robert M. Luscher, are similar to traditional Updike verities: the fear of death, finding personal identity through work, ambivalence about success, and the conflict between love and self-realization. [17] Such themes, played out in Henry Bech, can be Jewish or not.

Other themes in the Bech books seem quintessential-
ly Jewish. According to critic Malcolm Bradbury, Bech is "in
the tradition of Jewish-American modernism, in line with the
fiction of angst, alienation, and protest... He comes from the
counter-strand of American fiction, the dissenting immigrant,
anguished and extreme." [18]
    Pinsker agrees. Bech, he writes, "is the New York Jewish
intellectual writ large: guilt-ridden, ironic, half formed by literary modernism and the *Partisan Review*, half the captive of
traumatic childhood memory. In a word, he is alienated, ill at
ease in the larger America..." [19] Such trials of assimilation are,
of course, a traditional theme in immigrant literature, including Jewish-American writing.
    Jewish or not, are the Bech books worthy literature? Inev-
itably, they invite comparison to Updike's four Rabbit novels,
which were written about the same time. The Rabbit books
are the best-known of Updike's many novels, his most successful and most honored work. They, along with his brilliant short
stories of domestic life, guarantee Updike's reputation as one
of America's great writers – the natural heir, as Philip Roth has
observed, to Nathaniel Hawthorne's social realism of the 19th
century. [20]
    Rabbit gave Updike "a way in," he has said, "a ticket to the
America all around me." [21] Updike used that ticket to portray
the everyday-ness of his ordinary American Everyman. "What
I saw through Rabbit's eyes was more worth telling than what
I saw through my own," Updike has said. Through Rabbit's
eyes Bradbury writes, we see "the supermarket and the hamburger joint, the used car lot and the Toyota franchise, the

basketball court and the movie theater, the city and the suburban tract, the rolling superhighway and the wooded winding
back road..." [22]

Updike famously described his writing about ordinary life
as "giving the mundane its beautiful due." [23] But in Updike's
hands, the mundane was elevated to something sublime.

All of Rabbit's quotidian ordinariness is set against the 30-
year sweep of an America in the throes of radical change: the
innocence of the Eisenhower years, the Civil Rights Movement, the Apollo moonshot, the assassinations, the economic
challenge from Asia, and Reagan's America. Writes Bradbury:
"From life to death and from running to rest, (Rabbit) became
the hero of a long tale of middle-American life in the second
half of the 20th century, when America became a superpow-
er, commercialism became an outright ideology, sex became
a sport, goods and shopping became the only real culture." [24]

Beyond his penchant for social history, Updike was always
a very literary writer, who turned out serious criticism, poetry,
and essays. He never lost his passion for writing, his love of
the process, or the feel of books in his hand. So perhaps it is
not surprising that he needed another alter ego, a literary man
who was somehow different. And that was Henry Bech, a Jewish writer who came, by definition, from a very different world
than Rabbit Angstrom.

Adam Begley, who wrote a fine biography of Updike in 2014,
says Bech "represents a crucial part of his creator's personality
and experience." Harry Angstrom, the middle-American Everyman of the "Rabbit" novels, says Begley, " is a version of
what Updike might have been if he had never left Pennsylva-

nia; Bech is a version of what Updike might have been had he started out in New York and stubbornly stood his ground." [25] The Bech books, by critical consensus, don't measure up to Updike's best work. I agree. By design, they lack the broad sweep of the Rabbit novels, which I have always admired. Nor do they offer the distilled insight of the shrewdest short stories, especially the 20-year portrait of a marriage in the Maple stories. But today, so many years later, I find it a pleasure to re-read all the Bech books, a reminder of the brilliance of his writing, the smart glimpse into human relationships, the cleverness of the dialogue. They are funny, sometimes subtle, sometimes broad, a satiric look at writers and their follies. And, yes, they belong in the ranks of Jewish-American fiction. Updike, in his *goyish* fashion, succeeded in creating a memorable character – a writer who is Jewish in his own endearing way.

FOURTEEN

Cynthia Ozick:
Keeper of the Flame

Cynthia Ozick never won a National Book Award. She was never a finalist for the Pulitzer Prize. And she never made it into the Bellow, Malamud & Roth haberdashery. And yet she ranks right up there in the top tier of Jewish writers who gained preeminence in post-war America. Nearing 90, she's still at it.

I came to her late, in part because she herself was a late bloomer. She didn't publish her first novel, *Trust*, until 1966, when she was 37, and despite some strong reviews, it quickly disappeared. But, like Malamud, Ozick gained an early reputation with her short stories. And, like Mailer, she proved at least as good at essays and criticism as she was at fiction. To me, she became the most Jewish of the Jewish writers, dealing powerfully with Jewish identity in Diaspora America, as well as Holocaust themes. Ozick's Jewishness defined her literary persona.

Unlike Bellow and the other guys in the room, Ozick usually didn't mind being thought of as a Jewish writer. But she rebelled at being called a woman writer. When asked why one label was okay but not the other, she replied, with characteristic fierceness, that it was a "preposterous" question. "Jewish is a category of civilization, culture, and intellect. 'Women' is a category of anatomy and physiology. It's rough thinking to confuse vast cultural and intellectual movements with the capacity to bear children." [1]

Most of the writers who shunned the Jewish-American label – from Arthur Miller to Saul Bellow – feared that it would render their work parochial, lacking universal appeal. They generally saw it as a form of discrimination, a way of ghettoizing them, of limiting their readership. Not Ozick. She has defended the term "parochial" as a badge of honor. "All genius is parochial," she wrote in the *New York Times Book Review*. "Shakespeare wrote out of a tiny island, Yeats out of a still tinier one. Tolstoy had all the spaciousness of Russia, yet imagined the world mainly out of the French-speaking fraction of the Russian nobility." [2] And for good measure, she was fond of quoting Isaac Bashevis Singer's aphorism that every writer needs to have an address.[3]

Ozick's strong sense of Jewishness has led her to attack anything she thinks diminishes Jewish identity – or fails to honor its religious essence. She has become the defender of the faith, the keeper of the flame. And she brings an unrestrained fury to the task, an essayist's style that brooks no dissent. This gentle lady is a tough cookie, so much so that when novelist Zoe Heller reviewed Ozick's last collection of essays for the *New York Times*, she chided Ozick for the "aggressive snootiness of her tone...something unseemly and excessive." [4]

Thus, when John Updike, writing about Franz Kafka, said that Kafka "avoided Jewish parochialism," Ozick was quick to pounce: "Nothing could be more wrong-headed than this parched Protestant misapprehension of Mitteleuropa's tormented Jewish psyche...To belittle as parochial the cultural surround that bred Kafka is to diminish and disfigure the man..." Ozick also ridiculed the phrase "Kafkaesque" because it implied a fake universalism at the expense of Kafka the individual, whose writing stemmed from his unique circumstances, among them that he was a German-speaking Jew in pre-war Czechoslovakia. [5]

She had torn into Updike once before when he created Henry Bech, a secular Jewish writer modeled in part on Bellow, Malamud, Roth, and Mailer. When the first of Updike's three Bech novels appeared in 1970, Ozick wasted no time in calling Henry Bech an inauthentic Jew – "an imbecile to the core" – who was ignorant of the religion or the tradition. (See Chapter 14.)

Ozick's next target was William Styron, author of several significant novels, including *Lie Down in Darkness* and *The Confessions of Nat Turner*. In 1974, Styron wrote a piece in the *New York Times* called "Auschwitz's Message," in which he de-emphasized the central meaning of Auschwitz as a place dedicated to the genocide of Jews. "At Auschwitz not only Jews perished, but at least one million souls who were not Jewish," he wrote. Recalling a Catholic Polish woman he knew years before, a woman who lost her father, husband, and two children at Auschwitz, Styron said, "I cannot accept anti-Semitism as the sole touchstone by which we examine the monstrous paradigm that Auschwitz has become." And, he concluded, to take a "narrow view" of Nazi evil "is to ignore the ecumenical nature of that evil...If it was anti-Semitic, it was also anti-Christian...it was anti-human. Anti-life."[6]

In response, Ozick respectfully acknowledged that a million Christians were killed at Auschwitz along with 2.5 million Jews, but stated her argument with elegant bluntness: "The enterprise at Auschwitz was organized, clearly and absolutely, to wipe out the Jews of Europe. The Jews were not an *instance* of Nazi slaughter; they were the purpose and whole reason for it."[7]

Five years later, in *Sophie's Choice*, Styron made his own choice: he made the victim-protagonist of this Holocaust novel a Polish Gentile. "As a Jew, she would have been one more victim, and there wouldn't have been a novel," Styron said.[8] "She had to be a Christian" – a callous statement that suggests only Christian victims are worthy of artistic treatment. The novel thus pit Styron's conception of universal evil against the view that the Holocaust was genocide – specifically waged against Jews precisely because they were Jewish.

This time around, Ozick had plenty of company in the criticism of *Sophie's Choice*. Others claimed that Styron had "de-Judaized" Auschwitz [9], that he resorted to an "atypical" case [10], and that he blurred fact and fiction, thus falsifying history. But the criticisms didn't seem to matter much to readers or reviewers. *Sophie's Choice* quickly became an international best-seller and won the National Book Award in 1980, beating out Philip Roth's *The Ghost Writer*, which dealt with the Holocaust in its own brilliant way (See Chapter 12.) A film version of *Sophie's Choice* in 1982 was nominated for five Academy Awards, with Meryl Streep winning the best-actress Oscar for her portrayal of Sophie.

For what it's worth, I render a split decision in the fight over Styron's view of Auschwitz. Yes, many Christians were killed at Auschwitz, and we should remember and memorialize them. But, like Ozick, I think Styron was plainly wrong in his *New York Times* piece to slight the obvious truth that the Nazi concentration camps were explicitly built to exterminate European Jewry, and that they pretty much succeeded in their genocide. *Sophie's Choice* is another matter altogether, a work of imagination by a gifted novelist. Styron has written a powerful novel of one woman's unique suffering at the hands of the Nazis, and the success of the book and the movie further dramatized the horror of the Holocaust to millions of people.

Ozick wasn't deterred. In 1997, she went to war over the legacy of Anne Frank, insisting that the marketing of her famous diary, and especially the Broadway hit it became, have stripped Anne of her Jewishness and downplayed her suffering while hiding from the Nazis for two years in an Amsterdam attic. Instead, Ozick said, we were fed a kind of cockeyed optimism, a coming-of age story of a perky teenager. As Ozick wrote in *The New Yorker*: "A deeply truth-telling work has been turned into... the subversion of history." [11] (See Chapter 15.)

Ozick's own history very much defines who she is and why she feels so strongly about things Jewish. Her parents, Cecilia and William Ozick, were born in Russia at a time of frequent pogroms. At age five, her father was locked with other Jews in their community synagogue, while a mob gathered outside, threatening to burn it down. They were rescued by a priest from a neighboring village.[12] Her father emigrated to the United States when he was 21 to escape conscription by the Czarist regime. Her mother was already in the U.S., having emigrated when she was five.

As a child, Ozick wrote letters in Yiddish to her grandmother in Moscow. She recalled her grandmother's lullaby to her: "*Nikolay, Nikolay, oif dayn kop ikh shpay*, which means, "Czar Nicholas, I spit on your head."[13]

Later, she learned more distressing news about the fate of her Russian-born ancestors. "Not until I was grown up was I told about my great uncle Mottel and his son Raphael. In a pogrom in a Russian village, the Cossacks captured them and tied them to the tails of horses, upside down. The Cossacks galloped back and forth over the cobblestones until the heads were dashed to pieces. When at last my mother confessed this story, she whispered it."[14]

Mr. and Mrs. O, as they often addressed themselves, settled in the Pelham Bay section of the Bronx, where they ran the Park View Pharmacy, not far from where I grew up. As a girl, Cynthia delivered prescriptions in the neighborhood, a place she found "brutally difficult to be a Jew." She remembers stones being thrown at her and being called a Christ killer as she ran past two churches in her neighborhood. At Public School 71 in the Bronx, where she was the only Jewish student in her class, she was publicly "humiliated" when she refused to sing Christmas carols with her classmates.[15]

"I'm still hurt by P.S. 71," Ozick said decades later, when she was 61. "I had teachers who hurt me, who made me believe I was stupid and inferior." [16] Ozick thinks she was motivated to become a writer as "revenge against the book-hating, Jew-hating P.S. 71." [17]

The anti-Semitic trauma of her youth undoubtedly accounts for her fierce and long-standing defense of Judaism and Jewish culture. In his literary biography of Ozick, Victor Strandberg, an English professor at Duke University, says the incidents foreshadowed "a sometimes embittered lifelong struggle to valorize her own heritage against the annihilating ignorance of the majority culture." [18]

I can't help contrasting Ozick's childhood in the Bronx with my own. Her Pelham Bay neighborhood in the East Bronx is only about five miles away, as the pigeon flies, from my roots near Kingsbridge Road in the West Bronx. Yet, I experienced little of the anti-Semitism that so scarred her. For one thing, I lived in a very Jewish neighborhood, and nearly all the students at P.S. 86 were Jews. Perhaps more important, she went to elementary school in the 1930s, when anti-Semitism was rife, while I was a schoolboy in post-war America, when knowledge of the Holocaust tempered overt anti-Semitism.

Ozick escaped by attending Hunter College High School, an academically elite school in Manhattan, then only for girls, which enrolled many other Jewish students. But by then the U.S. was at war, raising other issues for a sensitive Jewish girl. "The dawning of what happened to the Jews of Europe came slowly...I am roughly the same age as Anne Frank...When I was blissful in high school, she was dying of typhus in Auschwitz." She has continued to express fury over the "atrocities" of the

20th century: "I confess that this is very central for me. I have an unending, unforgiving, implacable, self-devastating rage against Europe." [19]

She immersed herself in literature at NYU's Washington Square College, where she was an intense bookworm, graduating in 1949 with a Phi Beta Kappa key and an English honors thesis on the romantic poets: Blake, Coleridge, Wordsworth, and Shelley.

She went on to get a master's degree a year later from Ohio State. This time, her thesis was entitled "Parables in the Late Novels of Henry James." As she confessed in "The Lesson of the Master," an essay written in 1982, she "became Henry James" – a worshipper of what she called "high art" at the expense of living her life. [20] Back in New York, she tried writing a philosophical novel, with the working title of *Mercy, Pity, Peace, and Love*, which she abandoned after several years – "a long suck on that Mippel," [21] she has told several interviewers over the years. She then spent nearly seven years writing *Trust*, an erudite and ambitious novel with plenty of sex, social commentary, and Holocaust overtones. It won a few strong reviews, but had little impact. "Unreadable," she later said in an interview with *The Atlantic.* [22]

Ozick turned to short stories, which often won various literary prizes, and to essays, which ranged from literary concerns to Jewish issues. She preferred writing novels, but conceded her shortcomings: "I've been told my fiction is too intellectual – that one can't love the characters. I guess it's true, and I'm distressed by it." [23] In all, she has written six novels, seven collections of stories, and seven collections of essays.

In theory, at least, Ozick deplored fictionalizing the Holocaust, which amounts to "imagining those atrocities." Better, she has said, to read and understand the documents about the Holocaust, including the survivor reminiscences. She is "morally and emotionally opposed to the mytho-poeticization of these events in any form or genre. And yet, for some reason, I keep writing Holocaust fiction..." [24]

Much of her writing does indeed deal with the Holocaust, directly or indirectly. In *The Cannibal Galaxy* (1983), the protagonist is a Holocaust survivor who as a boy was hidden in a French cellar by nuns. *The Messiah of Stockholm* (1987) fictionalized the story of one of Ozick's literary heroes, Bruno Schulz, a writer killed by the Nazis. And her most recent novel, *Foreign Bodies* (2010), recast Henry James's *The Ambassadors* as a tale of American Jews in post-war Europe, the horror of the Holocaust lingering over them.

Perhaps her best-known piece of fiction is a short story published in *The New Yorker* in 1980 called *The Shawl*. It describes in chilling detail what happens to Rosa Lublin, an assimilated Polish Jew, in a Nazi concentration camp. Her baby, Magda, is murdered by a camp guard who throws the girl against an electric fence. In 1983, again in *The New Yorker*, Ozick published a sequel called *Rosa*, which takes place in Miami 30 years later. Rosa is now "a madwoman and a scavenger" surviving on "half a sardine or a small can of peas," and writing letters to her dead daughter Magda in "the most excellent literary Polish." For Rosa, the Holocaust never ended.

The two stories were published together in a single volume, *The Shawl*, in 1989, which was delayed because, Ozick said, she was immobilized by doubt about the "moral propriety" of making art out of the Holocaust. Today,[25] *The Shawl* is prominent on many college reading lists about the Holocaust, along with the work of Primo Levi and Elie Wiesel.

Ozick has described the experience of writing *The Shawl* as something she was driven to do. "I hate to say it," she told *The Guardian*. "It's the kind of absurd thing that I mock – that I wasn't writing it, that it was dictated..."[26]

Who dictated it to her? An inner voice that stems from the anti-Semitism she experienced as a young girl, her rage about the Holocaust, and her passionate belief in Judaism. "I don't want to tamper, or invent, or imagine [the Holocaust], and yet I have done it, she told the *Paris Review*. "I can't not do it. It comes. It invades."[27]

What are we to make of Ozick's role as defender of the faith, keeper of the flame of Judaism? Her religious views are central to her thinking. She has defined Jews as Biblical people who made a covenant with God – people chosen to show the world a monotheist God in return for a promised land. To be Jewish in Diaspora America, Ozick believes, a Jew must embrace the faith. "When a Jew becomes a secular person, he is no longer a Jew," she wrote.[28] And, naturally enough, she sees assimilation as a threat to Jewish survival.

Ozick's religiosity infused her view of literature as well. A Jewish writer, she has said, must be "liturgical," imbued with the creed of God's covenant. In a complex essay, "Toward a New Yiddish," written in 1970 and reprinted in 1983,[29] she lamented Philip Roth's statement that "I am not a Jewish writer; I am a writer who is a Jew." To Ozick, Roth's words "do not represent a credo; they speak for a doom." As she saw it, Roth was sacrificing the very parochialism and authenticity that is necessary for great literature. "There never yet lived a Jewish Dickens," Ozick declared. "There have been no literary giants in Diaspora...no Jewish Dante, or Shakespeare, or Tolstoy, or Yeats...Each was, if you will allow the infamous word, tribal. Literature does not spring from the urge to Esperanto but from the tribe...The annihilation of idiosyncrasy assures the annihilation of culture."

In case anybody missed the point, she singled out Norman Mailer, "born in the *shtetl* called Brooklyn...a tragic American exemplar of wasted power and large-scale denial." He will have his "three decades of Diaspora flattery," Ozick wrote, but he will end up as "a small Gentile footnote, about the size of H.L. Mencken." [30]

We don't yet know how history will judge Mailer, but Ozick was clearly wrong about Roth. Far from being doomed, Roth did his best work, some of it brilliant, in the years after Ozick doubted his future. Nor is it true that the Diaspora never bred a great Jewish writer, unless you're willing to ignore Kafka, Bellow, and Proust (who was half Jewish) and dismiss Roth. And, more broadly, does her definition of a Jew as a "covenanted" person, mean that only religious Jews can be Jewish? If so, I fail her test (see Chapter 16). In short, there's much to disagree with in Ozick's many essays written over many years, and I certainly do.

Yet, I often find Ozick's passion and deep religious feelings moving. She raises crucial issues of Jewish identity, she calls out people who deserve censure, and she knows in her head and heart that "Never Again" means "Never Forget." She has absorbed the lessons of Jewish history like few others, playing them back with a ferocious passion. Cynthia Ozick has become the literary messiah of Judaism.

Let us grant her the last word: "If we choose to be Mankind rather then Jewish...we will not be heard at all; for us, America will have been in vain." [31]

FIFTEEN

"Who Owns Anne Frank?"

All of Cynthia Ozick's fury and powerful writing came to the fore when she published a deeply reported piece, "Who Owns Anne Frank?" in *The New Yorker* in 1997.[1] Ozick took on the legacy of Anne Frank's famous diary, which has sold some 30 million copies in 67 different languages. "All in all," Ozick wrote, "the diary is a chronicle of trepidation, turmoil, alarm... It is a story of fear." But over the years it "has been bowdlerized, distorted, transmuted, traduced, reduced; it has been infantilized, Americanized, homogenized, sentimentalized, falsified, kitschified... Among the falsifiers and bowdlerizers have been dramatists and directors," including Anne Frank's own father, Otto Frank.

Ozick said Otto Frank helped create a shallow, upbeat view of the diary and the Broadway play that followed, aiming to emphasize "Anne's idealism," and "Anne's spirit"... "almost never calling attention to how that idealism and spirit were smothered, and generalizing the sources of hatred..."[2]

The diary's most famous line – "in spite of everything I still believe that people are really good at heart" – has been stripped of context, Ozick said, "torn out of its bed of thorns." Just two sentences later, Ozick pointed out, Anne wrote a much darker vision:

"I see the world gradually being turned into a wilderness, I hear the ever approaching thunder which will destroy us too. I can feel the suffering of millions..."[3]

Ozick is distressed that the "good-at-heart" line has become Anne Frank's posthumous message, "virtually her motto." After all, as Bruno Bettelheim observed years earlier, if people are truly good, Auschwitz never would have happened.[4] Asked Ozick: "Why should this sentence be taken as emblematic, and not, for example, another?" "There's in people simply an urge to destroy, an urge to kill, murder and rage..." Anne wrote in hiding on May 3, 1944. As Ozick put it: "These are words that do not soften, ameliorate, or give the lie to the pervasive horror of her time. Nor do they pull the wool over the eyes of history."[5]

How did Anne Frank's original and searing diary get so transformed in the public mind to so anger Ozick? It begins with Anne's father:

Otto Frank was a secular German Jew, an officer in the German Army in World War I, thoroughly assimilated, or so he thought, and well practiced in the art of accommodation. He was 44 when Hitler took power in Germany in 1933, and soon after he moved his family to Amsterdam, where he established a spice business. After the Nazis invaded the Netherlands, he took his family into hiding in July 1942, in attic rooms above his business office. Another Jewish family, called the Van Daans in the diary, went into hiding with them, along with a man named Dussel. After two years, they were apparently betrayed by an anonymous informer who was paid 7.5 guilders (about $1 at the time) for each Jew he turned in.[6] The Frank family was shipped to Auschwitz, and Otto Frank was the only survivor of the group in hiding. His wife Edith died in early 1945, while Anne and her older sister Margo were taken from Auschwitz to Bergen-Belsen in Germany, where they died of typhus in January 1945, just three months before the camp was liberated by Allied forces.

Because Anne's diary ended so abruptly, Ozick made sure in her *New Yorker* piece that people understood the horrifying details of Anne's annihilation. Ozick's account is based on the testimony of survivors, including Hannah Goslar, a former classmate of Anne's:

"[Anne] and her sister were among 3,659 women transported by cattle car from Auschwitz to the merciless conditions of Bergen-Belsen, a barren tract of mud. In a cold, wet autumn, they suffered through nights on flooded straw in overcrowded tents, without light, surrounded by latrine ditches, until a violent hailstorm tore away what had passed for shelter...Margot was the first to succumb. A survivor recalled that she fell dead to the ground from the wooden slab on which she lay, eaten by lice, and that Anne, heartbroken and skeletal, naked under a bit of rag, died a day or two later."[7]

Anne's diary was saved by Miep Gies, a Dutch woman, a Catholic member of the Dutch resistance, who worked at

Otto Frank's business and became one of the family's protectors when they were in hiding. After the war she gave the diary to Frank. He realized it was a story that had to be told.

But what story? Frank naturally wanted to portray Anne in the best possible light, a spunky, high-spirited teenager who made the best of it while hiding in an attic for two years before she was carted off to Auschwitz. So he edited her diary into a more palatable form, the better to appeal to a war-weary world eager for heroes and martyrs – a world seeking some consolation from the disastrous reality. Anne's diary, *The Secret Annex*, was published in Dutch in 1947 and translated into English in 1952 as *The Diary of a Young Girl*.

Eleanor Roosevelt provided an introduction to the American edition, probably ghost-written by the publisher, in which the words Jew or Jewish are never mentioned. Her plight is universalized, with such phrases as "an appropriate monument to her fine spirit and the spirits of those who have worked...for peace." In virtually every edition of the book over the years, Frank made sure the blurbs stressed things like "a song to life" or a "poignant delight in the infinite human spirit." The overall effect, Ozick writes, was to downplay reality: "The diarist's dread came to be described as hope, her terror as courage, her prayers of despair as inspiring..."

Not until the original and unexpurgated diary was finally published in 1991, eleven years after Frank's death, did we see what he had changed or omitted. He had dramatically softened Anne's teenage anger at her mother, downplaying the rupture in their relationship. He had cut Anne's explicit talk of her emerging sexuality. And even though the diary has many references to the family's Judaism and the Nazi's treatment of the Jews, Ozick said that Frank had "deleted numerous expressions of religious faith, a direct reference to Yom Kippur, terrified reports of Germans seizing Jews in Amsterdam." More than the original book, however, it was the Broadway play and subsequent movie that shaped the meaning and legend of Anne Frank, said Ozick. Renamed *The Diary of Anne Frank*, the play opened in 1955, adapted for the stage by the husband and wife team of Albert Hackett and Frances Goodrich. They were an unlikely pair for a Holocaust story, having written such light-hearted films as *Father of the Bride, It's a Wonderful Life, Easter Parade*, and *In the Good Old Summertime*. But they came highly recommended by Lillian Hellman, a successful Broadway playwright known for her Stalinist leanings and her anti-Zionism. The director was Garson Kanin, the producer was Kermit Bloomgarden, and Susan Strasberg, then 17, played Anne. Otto Frank approved the script.

Pushed by Hellman, as well as by Kanin and Bloomgarden, the writers created a script that Ozick said scrupulously downplayed "Anne's consciousness of Jewish fate or faith...Whatever was specific they made generic. The sexual tenderness between Anne and the young Peter van Daan was moved to the forefront. Comedy overwhelmed darkness. Anne became an all-American girl...The Zionist aspirations of Margot, Anne's older sister, disappeared." [8]

Kanin was blunt about his goal: "The fact that in this play the symbols of persecution and oppression are Jews is incidental..." In other words, said an equally blunt Ozick, "the particularized plight of Jews in hiding was vaporized" into a vague universalism that Kanin called the 'infinite."' [9]

The strategy worked: *Variety* said the play left "a glowing, moving, frequently humorous impression...It is not grim." And the *New York Daily News* said it was "not in any important sense a Jewish play...Anne Frank is a Little Orphan Annie brought into vibrant life." The play was a worldwide success – winner of the Pulitzer Prize for drama and mounted all over the world, from Israel to Germany. [10]

In short, just a decade after the fall of Nazi Germany, a decade after she died in Bergen-Belsen, Anne Frank was portrayed on Broadway in a sanitized fashion, devoid of the rage in her diary, her Jewishness minimized. The play became a secular ode to the human spirit, Ozick wrote, and Anne was little more than a generalized victim of mankind's inhumanity. "In a drama about hiding, evil was hidden." [11]

A Broadway revival in December 1997, starring 16-year-old Natalie Portman as Anne, was more faithful to the diary, restoring more of Anne's Jewishness and more of the tension in the attic, while retaining some of the humor and portraying Anne's coming-of age and sexual awakening. But even Natalie Portman said of Anne and the play: "It's funny, it's hopeful, and she's a happy person." [12]

That's not the way I remember it. I never saw the original 1955 production, but the 1997 revival left me sobbing and shaking, along with just about everybody else in the theater, when the Gestapo took them all away.

Ozick, upset at the misuse of Jewish identity and history, comes to a shocking conclusion. In the last paragraph of her essay she imagined a "more salvational" outcome: "Anne

Frank's diary burned, vanished, lost – saved from a world that made of it all things, some of them true, while floating lightly over the heavier truth of named and inhabited evil."

I understand Ozick's pain and anger at how the diary was misinterpreted by some and blatantly misused by others, but surely the world would not be a better place if the diary had been lost to us all, as Ozick fantasizes. After all these years, the indelible image of Anne rings loud and clear: the very human story of a teenager who hid in an attic for two years only to be murdered in a Nazi concentration camp because she was Jewish. And only because she was Jewish.

The enduring and tragic irony is that Anne Frank, dead at 15, became the most famous Jewish writer of them all.

SIXTEEN

What Kind of Jew Am I?

By Cynthia Ozick's definition, I am not Jewish. Though somewhat observant, I am more secular than religious, and Ozick has made it clear that she doesn't believe secular Jews are really Jewish. Is she right? Do you have to be religious to make the cut? That question, in turn, raises other questions, and I feel like the boy at the Passover *seder* who asks the Four Questions.

Here are mine: Just how religious do you have to be to satisfy Ozick's definition? If there's little or no religion in your life, what does it mean to be Jewish? Can you assimilate in diaspora America without losing your Jewishness? And, finally, will Judaism survive if a growing majority of young Jews not only assimilate but continue to intermarry?

I speak as a lapsed Jew who returned to the fold when I married Lynn. I reconnected not out of religious conviction. And not for the children, who were yet to be born. I did it partly to embrace my ancestry and cultural roots, to acknowledge my place as a secular Jew, but mostly I signed on because Lynn took her Jewishness seriously – showing reverence for the tradition and respect for the ritual. If it was important to her, it would be important to me. I didn't want to be left out.

After attending services at a few synagogues, we joined Rodeph Shalom, a reform temple, when Sarah and Ned went to nursery school there. But we soon switched to B'nai Jeshurun because Lynn wanted a conservative synagogue similar to the one she had attended with her family in Washington. And we very much liked B'nai Jeshurun's renaissance under Rabbi Marshall Meyer, who assumed the pulpit in 1985.

B'nai Jeshurun was founded in 1825, the second synagogue established in New York City and the third-oldest synagogue in the United States for Ashkenazi Jews (those from Eastern Europe). The present building, on the Upper West Side, was dedicated in 1918, but by the 1980s, when poverty and crime were rampant in the neighborhood, the congregation had shrunk to just 80 families.

Rabbi Meyer seemed heaven-sent to rebuild the congregation, and I admired what he stood for. He began attracting new members with his blend of social activism, spirited musical worship, and a vision of an open and inclusive community. He also invoked a strong commitment to a two-state resolution of the Middle East conflict. In effect, he created new priorities for the congregation, stressing his definition of what it meant to be Jewish: "Judaism that is not involved in social action is a contradiction in terms." [1]

Throughout his life, Marshall Meyer certainly practiced what he preached. Born in New York in 1930, he moved to

Argentina when he was 29, staying for 25 years and establishing a synagogue that now has the largest congregation in Latin America. He opposed the military dictatorship that seized power in 1976 and subsequently imprisoned or killed thousands of people – the so-called "disappeared." Despite threats to his family, Rabbi Meyer visited prisoners, regardless of their faith, and counseled their families. One former prisoner, Jacobo Timerman, dedicated his book, *Prisoner Without a Name, Cell Without a Number*, to Meyer, "a rabbi who brought comfort to Jewish, Christian, and atheist prisoners in Argentine jails." After the restoration of democracy in 1983, Rabbi Meyer served on a presidential commission in Argentina that traced 9,000 people and collected 50,000 pages of testimony on the role of the military regime. [2]

Two years later, he returned to New York to take charge of B'nai Jeshurun. Setting up shop up with a card table, a pay phone, and a roll of quarters, Rabbi Meyer moved quickly to enliven traditional religious services, bringing music and dancing to the Friday night services to embody the joy of Judaism. [3] (Not everyone appreciated all the music and singing at the expense of traditional decorum: Ozick, an Orthodox Jew, once called B'nai Jeshurun "the hootenanny on the Upper West Side.") [4]

More important than all the singing and dancing, Rabbi Meyer combined the ritual and the music with community outreach to promote social justice. One of his first steps was to establish a homeless shelter in the synagogue and a weekly meal for the hungry. [5] He soon broadened the synagogue's reach by welcoming gay congregants. He established interfaith ties to

Christian clergy and, when the synagogue's roof literally fell in, he conducted Rosh Hashanah and Yom Kippur services in nearby churches. (Such services continue to this day to accommodate B'nai Jeshurun's overflow crowds.) And to further the cause of peace in the Middle East, he invited Muslim speakers, and he himself criticized Israeli policy when the government wasn't living up to his ideals.

Rabbi Meyer's message was liturgical music to my secular ears. I embraced his vision of Judaism, especially his emphasis on social justice as a fundamental expression of Jewish belief. I loved it when he regularly challenged the Jewish establishment for its "conservatism," its reluctance to play a leadership role in fighting social and economic problems, as well as actively pursuing peace in the Middle East. And I was moved when he frequently quoted Isaiah: "Share your bread with the hungry, take the homeless into your home...Do not turn away from people in need."

Thanks in large measure to his extraordinary charisma and progressive policies, B'nai Jeshurun soon become a thriving liberal community that now has nearly 2,000 households as members, including our own. It has become a model for many other synagogues in the United States.[6] I had finally found my place, my comfort zone as a Jew.

Rabbi Meyer officiated at Sarah's Bat Mitzvah ceremony in November 1993, along with Cantor Ari Priven, who had worked with Rabbi Meyer in Argentina. The services were held in the Church of Saint Paul and Saint Andrew, where B'nai Jeshurun was in residence while it rebuilt the roof of its synagogue. Sadly, it was the last coming-of-age service presided over by Rabbi

Meyer. Six weeks later, he died of cancer at age 63. After his death, his rabbinic protégés from Argentina, Rolando Matalon and Marcelo Bronstein, along with a younger colleague, Rabbi Felicia Sol, extended the revitalization of B'nai Jeshurun. When Ned was ready for his Bar Mitzvah in 1995, Rabbi Matalon presided, with Cantor Priven. But the synagogue's roof still wasn't quite ready, so Ned's service was also held in the Church of Saint Paul and Saint Andrew. I've often thought that the Church setting for our children's Jewish rituals was apt symbolism for the ecumenical spirit our family shared with B'nai Jeshurun and its rabbis and cantor.

The congregation's emphasis on social justice persists to this day. At a recent Yom Kippur service, I was pleased to hear Rabbi Bronstein deliver a powerful sermon admonishing Jews who favored ritual over social action. He referred to a new book called Putting *God Second: How To Save Religion From Itself*, by Rabbi Donniel Hartman.[7] As the bold title declares, the book is a detailed argument against religious piety at the expense of actions that advance social and economic justice. I soon bought the book and read it carefully. Rabbi Hartman emphasized his point by frequently paraphrasing Hillel the Elder, the ancient Jewish sage: "What is hateful to you, do not do to your neighbor. That is the whole Torah. All of the rest is commentary..."

Lynn and I do observe some Jewish ritual. We light *Shabbos* candles on Friday nights, Lynn saying the blessing. I recite the Hebrew prayer over the wine, an ultra-sweet Manischewitz, and over the bread, a freshly baked *challah*. Sarah and Ned were always expected to eat dinner with us every Friday before scattering with their friends. Lynn urged them to invite their friends, Jewish or not, to Sabbath dinner, and they often did. We occasionally attend Friday night services, and Lynn is a regular on the high holidays of Rosh Hashonah and Yom Kippur. I join her for Kol Nidre services on Yom Kippur eve, the one service I genuinely find moving — mostly because it reminds me of sitting in *shul* with my father when I was a boy. We also host a break-the-fast gathering at our house every year for 40 or so friends and family — now part of our end-of-holiday tradition. Lynn has reason to celebrate: she fasts the entire day. I, however, do not.

Am I just going along for the ride? Well, mostly yes. Though I do feel a connection to Lynn's religiosity — and to 5,000 years of Jewish history — I am largely a secular Jew. But I've come to accept, as Sam Norich, president of *The Forward*, told me: "Being secular is as meaningful and compelling a way of being Jewish as the Orthodox black-hat way. It expresses fidelity to the Jewish people."[8]

I am hardly alone. In 2013, the Pew Research Center published the results of a comprehensive survey of American Jews.[9] "Secularism has a long tradition in Jewish life in America," the report said, "and most U.S. Jews seem to recognize this: 62% say being Jewish is mainly a matter of ancestry and culture, while only 15% say it is mainly a matter of religion." (The remaining 23% say it is both.) Even among religious Jews, more than half say being Jewish is mostly about ancestry and culture — and two-thirds say it is not even necessary to believe in God to be Jewish.[10]

The Pew report also probed the question of Jewish identity: "What does being Jewish mean in America today?" The answer: 73% of American Jews say "remembering the Holocaust" and 69% say "leading an ethical life." More than half say that "working for justice and equality is essential to what being Jewish means to them." Yet, whether religious or not, nearly all American Jews say they are proud to be Jews, and three out of four American Jews say they have "a strong sense of belonging to the Jewish people."

Naturally, I found the Pew report re-assuring. It placed me squarely in the mainstream of American Jewry, reinforcing my comfort level with my own Jewish identity. I didn't have to be religious to be Jewish. Culture matters a lot. So does social justice. So does Holocaust remembrance. And so does pride in being Jewish. It's okay, in short, to be a secular Jew. I was enormously pleased that I hadn't excommunicated myself from the tribe.

For all the camaraderie I found in the Pew report, a big question remains: Why remain Jewish if I have little feeling for the religious ritual? As the Pew report suggested, Jews like me harbor a powerful need to feel connected to a family, to a history, to ancestors, to a culture, to ethical responsibility, to a sense of belonging. Perhaps even to the literature that meant so much to me. Sigmund Freud, who was an atheist, called it a "the safe privacy of a common mental connection" [6] and Irving Kristol thought of it as an "intense Jewish secular humanism." [11] In short, Jews have been able to assimilate while still feeling strongly connected to the "peoplehood" of Jews.

And, of course, it wasn't just Jews. Because there were so many different immigrants from so many different countries and cultures, America generally accepted the idea of cultural pluralism. Jews were just another alien group in a melting pot that never really melted. The late Lawrence H. Fuchs, a scholar of American ethnicity at Brandeis University for 50 years, says this "voluntary pluralism" enabled immigrants from Europe to maintain affection for their ancestral religion and culture, while claiming an American identity by participating in its political life. Political participation, not religion, Fuchs says, was the central basis for citizenship. Groups of hyphenated Americans could thus become Americans while retaining much of their ethnic, religious, or cultural identity.[13]

Despite such assimilation, as my parents well knew, there was plenty of discrimination against the Jews, Irish, Italians, and other immigrants. Anti-Semitism in America was often vicious and widespread. It was only when the horror of the Holocaust was fully exposed that anti-Semitism in America slowly began to decline, eventually leading to something of a golden age for American Jews during the last 60 years or so. I was among the lucky beneficiaries, as were the many Jewish-American writers who emerged.

Lest we get complacent, the positive Jewish experience in post-war America has been marred recently by a rise in anti-Semitism, some of it linked to Israeli policy in the Middle East and some linked to the white supremacist "alt-right" movement in America, enabled by the rise of Donald Trump and his former chief strategist, Stephen Bannon. But by historical comparison, anti-Semitic incidents in the U.S. are still few, at least so far.

While American Jews have Americanized in many ways, we

have managed to retain a distinctively Jewish way of thinking, consistent with our emphasis on social justice. Like me, most American Jews have adopted strong progressive values. We are more accepting of gay rights, abortion rights, immigration, and gun control than the general populace, and less willing to endorse school prayer or capital punishment.[14] In our politics, American Jews are reliably Democratic, voting twice for Barack Obama by huge margins (above 70% both times)[15] and overwhelmingly rejecting Donald Trump in 2016 (about 71% of Jews voted for Hillary Clinton.)[16]

Much of this is based on values that stem from centuries of Jewish thought embodied by the Hebrew phrases *tikkun olam*, which means repair of the world, or *tzedakah*, a single word that means both justice and charity. Rabbi Abraham Joshua Heschel has pointed out that a key word in Christianity is "salvation," which requires faith in an afterlife. In Judaism, there is a concept of the afterlife, but it is downplayed in favor of an emphasis on perfecting the earthly world. Thus, Jews talk of "*mitzvah*," which means good deeds done in the life we live here and now.

Like me, most Jews also stress the importance of education, and the roots of this thinking are decidedly religious. In 64 CE, Rabbi Joshua Ben Gamla mandated universal schooling for all Jewish boys starting at age six – at a time when nearly everyone else in the world was illiterate. Why? To enable them to read the Torah and the Talmud[17] and transmit their wisdom to the next generations – which, quite naturally, helped to preserve Judaism over the centuries. Among American Jews, many of them secular, learning has become "a metaphor for worship," says former Swarthmore Professor Richard R. Rubin.[18]

As a result, Jews in America are among the most highly educated fraction of the citizenry. According to the Pew report, 58% of American Jews have graduated from college, including 28% who have completed post-graduate study – both levels at least double those in the population at large.[19] Such educational achievement has resulted in worldly success and acclaim for many Jews, disproportionate to their numbers, especially in the professions.

In discussing such matters, it is easy to fall into the trap of Jewish exceptionalism – the concept of "the chosen people" taken to a triumphalist and sacrilegious extreme.[20] We Jews, the obvious must be said, are hardly the only people who care about education, social justice, or charity – or who supported Barack Obama and rejected Donald Trump. Christian clergy have preached charity and social justice while spurring social action for generations, starting long before there were enough Jews in America to form a *minyan*. And whatever disproportionate success Jews have achieved, we remain a tiny minority among the millions of well-educated, successful Americans from all walks of life, from all religions, from all ethnic backgrounds. Pride is fine, arrogance isn't.

For all the acceptance we've gained, American Jews today are facing existential questions: Will our distinctiveness as Jews survive over many more generations as the bond of religion continues to weaken? Will a common ancestry be enough as memories of immigrant life and even of the Holocaust fade? Will secular humanism be enough? Will a common culture? Will liberal political views? Will a connection to Israel? What, in short, will be the glue that continues to bind us as Jews? These questions take on a critical urgency because of the high rate of intermarriage between Jews and Christians. Once, it was considered a *shonda*, a disgrace, if Jews married out of the faith – the stuff of dramatic tension in Jewish life, literature, and theater. (*Fiddler on the Roof*, anyone?) Today, it's an everyday thing. Among all Jews who have married since 2000, 58% have wed non-Jews. If you exclude Orthodox Jews, the intermarriage rate is 70% – a startling rise from the 1960s, when only 17% of Jews married non-Jews.[21] In many mixed marriages, according to the Pew study, more than one-third of the children are not raised as Jews in any way.[22]

It doesn't take much imagination to see where this leads. Cynthia Ozick has always viewed assimilation as a threat to Jewish survival – hence her disdain for secular Jews – and the high rate of intermarriage is a clear and present danger. It's possible, perhaps even likely, that the traditional Jewish values of social justice, education, liberalism, and the rest, will be passed on to the non-Jewish children and grandchildren of intermarried couples – and that the legacy of Judaism will be sustained even as the religious faith continues to decline.

But, in the spirit of the Talmud, we must ask: Will mainstream Judaism collapse without its religious core? Is secularism gradually doing what centuries of anti-Semitism couldn't do: undermining the peoplehood of Jews, those of us who happen to live in America?

I pray the answer is no.

Epilogue

The post-war heyday of the Jewish-American writer peaked in the 1950s and 1960s, and lasted well into the 1980s and 1990s. Cynthia Ozick, 89, is still at it, but Philip Roth, Bruce Jay Friedman, and Herbert Gold have retired from writing and nearly all of the other pioneers are dead, including Saul Bellow, Bernard Malamud, Norman Mailer, Arthur Miller, E.L. Doctorow, Joseph Heller, J.D. Salinger, and Grace Paley. They overcame a lot of prejudice, broke new ground in American fiction, reached millions of readers, and won all the major literary prizes. The pioneers did what pioneers always do: they led the way, in this case to a literary promised land.

The pioneers made a real difference to me. I encountered many memorable Jewish characters along the way – from Herzog to Portnoy, from Augie to Dubin, from Morris Bober to Rosa Lublin, from Herman Broder to Henry Bech. Through them, I was able to contemplate my own Jewish identity – sometimes quite consciously, more often surfaced from the deeper world of my inner life. I came to better understand my own family background, and I was able to keep open the door to my eventual return to Judaism. Aided by Lynn's more observant embrace of the religion, I was finally able and willing to come to terms with my own Jewishness.

My re-reading of these books so many years later has deepened my understanding of them, and of myself. Roth, if anything, felt better than ever, showing great range and poignance, especially in his later books. More than the others, he seemed to speak to me and my generation about our concerns. Bellow, for all his psychological insight and ironic humor, seemed somewhat diminished, lacking the story-telling skills of, say, Isaac Bashevis Singer. Malamud? He helped me understand deep suffering, Jewish or otherwise. And Ozick, though irritating in her strident certainties and narrow definition of Judaism, challenged my easy assumptions about being Jewish – and reinforced the powerful feelings about the Holocaust that I first experienced as a child.

As often happens when an era ends, we now have biographies and memoirs of most of the major players. Roth's biography, by Blake Bailey, is in the works, as is Doctorow's, by Bruce Weber. But the lives of Bellow, Malamud, and Singer are well chronicled, and Miller wrote his own biography.[1]

What we see is the struggle all of them had: Bellow to overcome anti-Semitism; Malamud to save his mother from suicide, overcome poverty, and help his brother with lifelong depression; Miller to deal with the Depression-era bankruptcy of his father that upended the family; and Singer to start anew as a Polish immigrant to America. I found that their life stories enriched my own journey and deepened my appreciation of their work.

And I came to realize, with sadness, that I just don't have the same passion for today's Jewish writers. It's not that they aren't writing good fiction. I especially admire the work of Michael Chabon, who won the Pulitzer Prize in 2001 for his novel, *The Amazing Adventures of Kavalier & Clay*, a tour-de-force about two Jewish cousins who created super-hero comic books in the years leading up to World War II. Other writers of note include Nathan Englander, Jonathan Safran Foer, Allegra Goodman, Dara Horn, Nicole Krauss, and Ayelet Waldman.

What's different now? Most obviously, I didn't come of age reading these writers. I no longer need fiction to mediate my struggle with my own Jewishness, the sense of victimization I absorbed from my family. I no longer need a Bellow or Roth to think about what kind of Jew I was or wanted to be. I no longer need an Ozick to defend the faith of Judaism or to help me contemplate the horror of the Holocaust in new ways. And, of course, times changed: I matriculated into a world remarkably free of the discrimination that plagued my parents' generation – a world that allowed me opportunities they never had.

In short, I don't depend on this new cohort of writers to shore me up, broaden the narrow horizon of my youth, or even instill pride. Unless it is especially relevant, I don't really care much whether or not they are Jewish. I do, however, very much care about the quality of what they write.

I find myself thinking again about Saul Bellow, the patriarch who bore the brunt of the early discrimination against Jewish writers. I'm glad he lived to see the day when Jewish writers generally came to be regarded the way he always thought was proper: They are writers who just happen to be Jewish.

Notes

PROLOGUE

1. J.D. Salinger's father, Sol Salinger, was Jewish, the son of a rabbi who became a doctor. J.D.'s mother, Marie Jillich was a Gentile from Iowa. After she married Sol, she changed her name to Miriam and considered herself Jewish. According to the Jewish Virtual Library, J.D. Salinger didn't know of his mother's Christian roots until after he had his Bar Mitzvah. As an adult, Salinger showed no interest in Judaism, preferring instead Eastern religions such as Buddhism and Hinduism. See "Salinger: A Life," by Kenneth Slawenski, Random House, 2010.

CHAPTER 1 WHAT'S HE GONNA DO, OPEN A HISTORY STORE?"

1. Saul Bellow, "Starting Out In Chicago," *American Scholar*, Winter 1974-1975. Bellow's full quote: "I am often described as a Jewish writer; in much the same way one might be called a Samoan astronomer or an Eskimo cellist or a Zulu Gainsborough expert."

2. Hermione Lee, "Philip Roth: The Art of Fiction No. 84," *The Paris Review*, Issue 93, Fall 1984. Roth was speaking generally about the Jewish quality in his books, and he cited a specific book as an example: The Anatomy Lesson.

3. Irving Howe, World of Our Fathers, Harcourt Brace Jovanovich, 1976.

4. Irving Howe, "Life Never Lets Up," *The New York Times Book Review*, October 25, 1964.

5. For a largely favorable review of the four novels collectively titled Mercy of a Rude Stream, see "A Prodigal Struggle With Demons," by Nathaniel Rich, *New York Review of Books*, April 23, 2015.

6. Steven G. Kellman, Redemption: The Life of Henry Roth, W.W. Norton, 2005.

7. "Rise of David Levinsky," *The New York Times Book Review*, September 16, 1917.

8. Saul Bellow, "Up From the Pushcart," *The New York Times Book Review*, January 15, 1961.

CHAPTER 2 MY JEWISH AWAKENING

1. *Life* magazine, May 7, 1945. Margaret Bourke-White, William Vandivert, and other Life photographers accompanied General George Patton's Third Army when it liberated Buchenwald, Bergen-Belsen, and other concentration camps in Germany in April 1945. Their photographs were among the first to document the Nazi killing fields to a stunned world. For its 25th anniversary issue, December 26, 1960, *Life* published still more of the original photographs.
2. Lynn Povich, *The Good Girls Revolt*, Public Affairs, 2012.
3. Shirley Povich, All Those Mornings at the Post, edited by Lynn, Maury, and David Povich and George Solomon. Public Affairs. 2005.
4. The names of these villages in pre-war Europe are frequently spelled in different ways. Kolomaya is often rendered Kolomea, Kolomai, or Kolomyya. And Suwalki is sometimes spelled Suvalk. See, for example, Chester G. Cohen, Shtetl Finder Gazetteer, Heritage Books, 2007.

CHAPTER 3 JEW VS. JEW: PHILIP ROTH'S *ELI, THE FANATIC*

1. "The Jewish Community Study of New York: 2011," sponsored by the UJA-Federation of New York. The study covers the five boroughs of New York City, plus Westchester, Nassau and Suffolk counties. It does not include New Jersey or Connecticut.
2. Of the total number of Orthodox Jews in the New York area, more than two-thirds belong to ultra-orthodox sects, such as the Hasidic (48.5%) and the Yeshivish (19.7%). The remaining 31.8% are modern orthodox Jews.
3. "The Yeshiva Comes To Westchester: The Legalistic Hedges of Suburbia," by Herrymon Maurer, *Commentary*, April 1949.
4. Josh Nathan-Kazis, "How Donald Trump Swept Orthodox Brooklyn – And Blocked A Democratic Landslide for Democrats," *Forward*, November 10, 2016.

CHAPTER 4 GANSEVOORT STREET: THE WORLD OF *OUR* FATHERS

1. Gansevoort Street was originally an Indian footpath to the Hudson River, the same route it has today. In the 18th and 19th century, it was unofficially called the Great Kiln Road, after the many furnaces in the area that turned oyster shells from the Hudson into a kind of mortar that was used by bricklayers. In 1811, anticipating war with

Britain, the city created landfill at the Hudson end of Great Kiln Road and built a fort, which was named Gansevoort Fort in honor of Peter Gansevoort, a hero of the Revolutionary War (and much later the grandfather of Herman Melville). The fort was torn down in the 1840s, but the street was renamed for Peter Gansevoort in 1937, about the time my father went to work at Number 40.

2. "Back to the Soil: The Jewish Farmers of Clarion, Utah, and Their World," by Robert Alan Goldberg, University of Utah Press, Salt Lake City, 1986. "Echoes of Jewish Back-to-Land Movement Under Utah's Big Sky," by Naomi Zeveloff plus accompanying video, "Utah's Jewish Pioneer." Forward, September 16, 2011.

3. "Borough of Roosevelt Historical Collection: History Of Roosevelt, New Jersey." Rutgers University Library. "From the Jersey Homesteads to Roosevelt: Community and Identity in a New Deal Settlement," by Kimberly A. Brodkin, American History Senior Honors Thesis, University of Pennsylvania, March 1992.

4. Author conversation with Don Brown, March 14, 2016.

5. Bib Brown Interview with step-daughter, Sarah Michaels, August 1999.

6. Ibid.

7. Author conversations with Don Brown, May 10, 2016 and June 9, 2016.

8. Ibid.

9. Ibid.

CHAPTER 5 IS WILLY LOMAN JEWISH? DOES IT MATTER?

1. Morris Freedman, *American Drama In Social Context*, Southern Illinois University Press, 1971.

2. Debra Caplan, Baruch College, program notes for Yiddish Rep production of *Death of a Salesman in Yiddish*, Castillo Theatre, 543 West 42nd St., New York, NY, October 8 – November 22, 2015.

3. George Ross, "On the Horizon: Death of a Salesman in the Original," *Commentary*, February 1, 1951.

4. New Yiddish Rep in association with Castillo Theatre, *Death of a Salesman in Yiddish*, Castillo Theatre, New York, October 8-November 22, 2015.

5. Leslie A. Fiedler, *Waiting For the End*, Stein and Day, 1964.

6. David Mamet, *The Human Stain*, *The Guardian*, May 6, 2005.

7. *Arthur Miller Centennial Event*, Symphony Space, New York, October 22, 2015.

8. 1969 interview by Robert A. Martin, collected by Matthew Charles Roudan in *Interviews With Arthur Miller*, University Press of Mississippi, 1987.

9. Julius Novick, *Beyond the Golden Door: Jewish American Drama and Jewish American Experience*, Palgrave Macmillan, 2008.

10. Fiedler, *Waiting for the End.*

11. Mary McCarthy, *Sights and Spectacles: Theater Chronicles, 1937-1956*, Meridian Books, 1957.

12. Novick, *Beyond the Golden Door.*

13. Christopher Bigsby, *Arthur Miller, 1915- 1962*, Harvard University Press, 2009. Page 325.

14. Arthur Miller, *Timebends: A Life*, Grove Press, 1987. Pages 126-131.

15. Arthur Miller, preface to *Death of a Salesman*, 50th anniversary edition, Penguin Books, 1999.

16. Arthur Miller, *Timebends*. Page 70.

17. Ibid. Page 36.

18. Ibid. Page 24.

19. Ibid. Page 71.

20. Marilyn Berger, "Arthur Miller, Moral Voice Of American Stage, Dies at 89," New York Times, February 12, 2005.

21. Bigsby, Arthur Miller, 1915-1962. Page 38.

22. Miller, *Timebends*. Page 117.

23. Ibid. Page 114.

24. Ibid. Page 115.

25. *Arthur Miller Centennial Event*, Symphony Space, New York, October 22, 2015.

26. Miller, *Timebends*. Page 547.

CHAPTER 6 MY ENCOUNTER WITH ISAAC BASHEVIS SINGER

1. Samuel G. Freedman, "Classes in Judaic Studies, Drawing a Non-Jewish Class," *The New York Times*, November 3, 2004.
2. Janet Hadda, *Isaac Bashevis Singer: A Life*, Oxford University Press, 199. Hadda died in 2015.
3. Dvorah Telushkin, *Master of Dreams: A Memoir of Isaac Bashevis Singer*, Perennial, 2004.

CHAPTER 7 THE IMMIGRANTS FROM KOLOMAYA

1. Eileen Lebow, *The Bright Boys: A History of Townsend Harris High School*, Greenwood Publishing Group, 2000.
2. *City College Department of Physics Newsletter, Volume 6, Fall. 2006.* Commemoration of the 85th anniversary of Einstein's visit to CCNY, where he gave six lectures.
3. Townsend Harris High School re-opened in 1984 and is now affiliated with Queens College, part of the CUNY system.

CHAPTER 8 EIGHT GUYS READING SAUL BELLOW

1. Philip Roth, *Shop Talk: A Writer and his Colleagues and Their Work*, Vintage Books, 2001.
2. Philip Roth, "Imagining Jews," *Reading Myself and Others*, Farrar, Straus & Giroux, 1975.
3. Ernest Hemingway: *The Sun Also Rises* and *A Farewell to Arms*. F. Scott Fitzgerald: *The Great Gatsby* and *Tender is the Night*. William Faulkner: *The Sound and the Fury*. Virginia Woolf: *Mrs. Dalloway* and *To the Lighthouse*. Henry Roth: *Call It Sleep*. Saul Bellow: *The Adventures of Augie March*, *Seize The Day*, and *Herzog*. Bernard Malamud: *The Assistant* and *The Magic Barrel*. Philip Roth: *The Ghost Writer* and *Exit Ghost*. E.L. Doctorow: *Ragtime* and *The Book of Daniel*. James Joyce: *Dubliners* and *A Portrait of the Artist As A Young Man*. George Eliot: *Middlemarch*. Mark Twain: *The Adventures of Huckleberry Finn*. James Baldwin: *Go Tell It on a Mountain*. Richard Wright: *Native Son*. Ralph Ellison: *Invisible Man*.
4. Robert Gorham Davis, "Augie Just Wouldn't Settle Down," *The New York Times Book Review*, September 20, 1953.
5. Joan Acocella, "Finding Augie March," *The New Yorker*, October 6, 2003.

6. Jack Rosenthal, a good friend to many of us, was diagnosed with pancreatic cancer a year later, and died on August 23, 2017. See his obituary: Sam Roberts, "Jack Rosenthal, Times Journalist and Civic Leader, Is Dead At 82," *The New York Times*, August 24, 2017. See also, Stephen B. Shepard, "Jack Rosenthal: An Appreciation," *The Forward*, August 24, 2017.

7. Alfred Kazin, "In Search of Light," *The New York Times*, November 18, 1956.

8. V.S. Pritchett, "King Saul," *New York Review of Books*, October 22, 1964.

9. Irving Howe, "Odysseus, Flat On His Back," *New Republic*, September 19, 1964.

10. Zachary Leader, *The Life of Saul Bellow, 1915-64*, Alfred A. Knopf, 2015.

Chapter 9 Literary Anti-Semitism

1. Michiko Kakutani, "A Talk With Saul Bellow: On His Work and Himself," *The New York Times*, December 13, 1981.

2. Ibid.

3. Zachary Leader, *The Life of Saul Bellow, 1915-64*, Alfred A. Knopf, 2015.

4. Ben Siegel, "Bellow As Jew and Jewish Writer," Chapter 2, *A Political Companion to Saul Bellow*, edited by Gloria Cronin and Lee Trepanier. University Press of Kentucky, 2013.

5. James Atlas, *Bellow: A Biography*, Random House, 2000.

6. Katherine Anne Porter, interviewed by Hank Lopez, "A Country and Some People I Love," *Harper's* magazine, September 1965.

7. Ibid.

8. "Playboy Interview: Truman Capote," *Playboy* magazine, March 1968.

9. Ibid.

10. Gore Vidal, "Literary Gangsters," *Commentary*, March 1970.

11. Ibid.

Chapter 10 Philip Roth's Turning Point

1. *Letting Go* (1962) and *When She Was Good* (1967).

2. *Our Gang* (1971), *The Breast* (1972), *The Great American Novel* (1973), *My Life as a Man* (1974), and *The Professor of Desire* (1977).

3. Claudia Roth Pierpont, *Roth Unbound*, Farrar, Straus & Giroux, 2013

4. Edwin McDowell, "Publishing: Pulitzer Controversies," *New York*

Times, May 11, 1984.

5. Claudia Roth Pierpont, *Roth Unbound.*

6. Philip Roth, *The Facts: A Novelist's Autobiography*, Farrar, Straus & Giroux, 1988.

7. After *The Ghost Writer*, Roth deployed Zuckerman as a narrator in eight more novels: *Zuckerman Unbound, The Anatomy Lesson, The Prague Orgy, The Counterlife, American Pastoral, I Married a Communist, The Human Stain,* and *Exit Ghost.*

8. Philip Roth, *The Facts.*

9. Philip Roth, *The Facts.*

10. Michael Rothberg, "Roth and the Holocaust," *The Cambridge Companion to Philip Roth*, edited by Timothy Parrish, Cambridge University Press, 2007.

11. Quoted by Philip Roth in *Reading Myself and Others.*

12. Philip Roth, *The Facts.*

13. Ibid.

14. Ibid.

15. Ibid.

16. Philip Roth, When She Was Good, Random House, 1967.

17. Philip Roth, *Reading Myself and Others.*

18. The movie version of *Goodbye, Columbus* was released by Paramount in April 1969. Written by Arnold Schulman and directed by Larry Peerce, it starred Ali MacGraw as Brenda Patimkin and Richard Benjamin as Neil Klugman.

19. Philip Roth, *Reading Myself and Others.*

20. Ibid.

21. Josh Greenfield, "Portnoy's Complaint," *New York Times*, February 23, 1969.

22. Philip Roth, *Reading Myself and Others.*

23. "All Time 100 Novels," *Time*, October 16, 2005.

24. Claudia Roth Pierpont, *Roth Unbound.*

25. Unlike Zuckerman's father, Roth's own parents always supported his work, claiming that the fuss it caused among some Jews was much ado about nothing.

26. Michael Rothberg, "Roth and the Holocaust."

27. Roth himself didn't have prostate cancer, though he did have many health problems over the years—including a burst appendix that almost killed him, chronic back pain, serious depression, and quintuple heart bypass surgery.

28. By invoking incest, Roth is likening Lonoff to Henry Roth, author of the legendary 1934 novel, *Call it Sleep*, who 60 years later admitted he had an incestuous relationship with his sister.

29. Robert McCrum, "Bye-bye ... Philip Roth Talks of Fame, Sex and Growing Old in Last Interview," *The Guardian*, May 17, 2014.

CHAPTER 11 BERNARD MALAMUD: THE FORGOTTEN MAN

1. Israel Shenker, "After Portnoy, What?" *New York* magazine, May 20, 1969.

2. Harry Sylvester, "With Greatest of Ease," book review of *The Natural*, *The New York Times*, August 26, 1952.

3. TriStar Pictures released May 11, 1984. Directed by Roger Levinson, written by Roger Towne and Phil Dusenberry. Starring Robert Redford as Roy Hobbs.

4. Philip Roth, "Pictures of Malamud," *The New York Times*, April 20, 1986.

5. Richard Lacayo, "All-Time 100 Novels," *Time* magazine, January 6, 2010.

6. Saul Bellow letter to Harvey Swados, September 28, 1961. Reprinted in *Saul Bellow Letters*, edited by Benjamin Taylor, Viking Penguin, 2010.

7. Mervyn Rothstein, "Bernard Malamud Dies at 71," *The New York Times*, March 19, 1986.

8. Janna Malamud Smith, *My Father Is A Book*, Houghton Mifflin Co., 2006.

9. Philip Davis, *Bernard Malamud: A Writer's Life*, Oxford University Press, 2007.

10. Cynthia Ozick, "Judging The World," *The New York Times Book Review*, March 16, 2014.

11. Philip Davis, *Bernard Malamud: A Writer's Life*.

12. Janna Malamud Smith, *My Father Is A Book*.

13. Michiko Kakutani, "Malamud Still Seeks Balance and Solitude," *The New York Times*, July 15, 1980.

14. Janna Malamud Smith, *My Father Is A Book*.

15. Philip Roth, "Pictures of Malamud."

16. Janna Malamud Smith, *My Father Is A Book*.

17. Amazingly enough, according to Davis's biography, Harcourt Brace turned down Malamud's next book, *The Assistant*, and Giroux, who

had moved from Harcourt to Farrar, Straus, promptly snapped it up. Farrar, Straus (later renamed Farrar, Straus & Giroux) published all the rest of Malamud's books.

18. Philip Davis, *Bernard Malamud: A Writer's Life*. The lifelong friend was Herbert Witkin.

19. Mervyn Rothstein, "Bernard Malamud Dies at 71."

20. Farrar, Straus & Giroux paperback edition, 2003.

21. Philip Roth, "Imagining Jews," *New York Review of Books*, September 29, 1974.

22. Philip Roth, "Pictures of Malamud," *The New York Times*, April 20, 1986.

23. For slightly different accounts of the Roth-Malamud flap, see "Pictures of Malamud," by Philip Roth and *My Father Is A Book*, by Janna Malamud Smith.

24. Janna Malamud Smith, *My Father Is A Book*.

25. Ruth Wisse, The Modern Jewish Canon, The Free Press, 2000.

26. Ibid.

27. Philip Davis, *Bernard Malamud: A Writer's Life*.

28. Morris Dickstein, "The Toils of Bernard Malamud," *Times Literary Supplement*, May 12, 2006.

29. Cynthia Ozick, "Judging The World."

30. Saul Bellow, letter to Harvey Swados, September 28, 1961.

31. Philip Davis, *Bernard Malamud: A Writer's Life*.

32. Ibid.

33. Author conversation with Bert Pogrebin, November 9, 2016.

34. Janna Malamud Smith, *My Father Is a Book*.

35. Philip Davis, *Bernard Malamud: A Writer's Life*.

36. Ibid.

37. Ibid.

38. Ibid.

39. Philip Roth, "Pictures of Malamud," *The New York Times*, April 20, 1986.

CHAPTER 12 GREENHORNS AND YANKEES

1. Cited in "The Bums Are Still a Rush," by Mark Starr, *Newsweek*, July 11, 2007.

CHAPTER 13 THE JEWISH JOHN UPDIKE

1. John Updike, "Hub Fans Bid Kid Adieu," *The New Yorker*, October 22, 1960. Issued as a hardcover book with the same title by Library of America, April 29, 2010, the 50th anniversary of Ted Williams' last day at Fenway Park.
2. John Updike, "The Bulgarian Princess," *The New Yorker*, March 13, 1965.
3. John Updike, "One Big Interview," in *Picked-Up Pieces*, Alfred A. Knopf, 1975.
4. Robert Detweiler, *John Updike*, Twayne Publishers, 1972.
5. Adam Begley, *Updike*, Harper Collins, 2014.
6. Charlie Riley, "A Conversation With John Updike," published in *Conversations With John Updike*, edited by James Plath, 1978. Reprinted in *John Updike: A Study of the Short Fiction*, by Robert A. Luscher, Twayne Publishes, 1993.
7. John Updike, "One Big Interview."
8. Harold Bloom, "Introduction," *Modern Critical Views of John Updike*, edited by Harold Bloom, Chelsea House, 1987.
9. Norman Podhoretz, "A Dissent on Updike," Commentary, 1963. Reprinted in *Doings and Undoings: The Fifties and After in American Writing*, Farrar, Straus & Giroux, 1966.
10. Paul Gray, "Perennial Promises Kept: For John Updike at 50, Bech Tops Off A Very Good Year," *Time*, October 18,1982.
11. Richard Burgin, "A Conversation With John Updike," *John Updike Newsletter*, No. 10 and 11, Spring and Summer, 1979. Reprinted in *John Updike's Novels*, by Donald Greiner, Ohio University Press, 1984.
12. Frank Gaddo, "Interview With John Updike," *First Person: Conversations on Writers and Writing*, Union College Press, 1973.
13. Paul Gray, *Time*.
14. Cynthia Ozick, "Bech, Passing," *Commentary*, November 1970. Reprinted in Art & Ardor, Alfred A. Knopf, 1983.
15. Cynthia Ozick, *Art & Ardor*.
16. Sanford Pinsker, "Updike, Ethnicity, and Jewish-American Drag," *The Cambridge Companion to John Updike*, edited by Stacey Olster, Cambridge University Press, 2005.
17. Robert A. Luscher, *John Updike: A Study of the Short Fiction*, Twayne Publishes, 1993.
18. Malcolm Bradbury, "Introduction," *The Complete Henry Bech*, Every-

man's Library, Alfred A. Knopf, 2001.

19. Sanford Pinsker, "John Updike and the Distractions of Henry Bech, Professional Writer and Amateur American Jew," *Modern Fiction Studies*, Volume 37, Number 1, Spring 1991, Johns Hopkins University Press.

20. Christopher Lehmann-Haupt, "John Updike, a Lyrical Writer of the Middle-Class Man, Dies at 76," *The New York Times*, January 28, 2009.

21. Malcolm Bradbury, *The Complete Henry Bech*.

22. Ibid.

23. John Updike, "Forward," *The Early Stories, 1953-1975*, Alfred A. Knopf, 2003.

24. Malcolm Bradbury, *The Complete Henry Bech*.

25. Adam Begley, *Updike*.

CHAPTER 14 CYNTHIA OZICK – KEEPER OF THE FLAME

1. "The Many Faces of Cynthia Ozick." Interview in *The Atlantic*, May 15, 1997.

2. Cynthia Ozick, "Hanging The Ghetto Dog," *New York Times Book Review*, March 21, 1976.

3. Cynthia Ozick, "Traditions and (or Versus) the Jewish Writer" in *Who We Are: On Being (and Not Being) A Jewish American Writer*, edited by Derek Rubin, Schocken Books, 2005.

4. Zoe Heller, "Cynthia Ozick Takes Up Arms Against Today's Literary Scene," *New York Times Book Review*, July 13, 2016.

5. Cynthia Ozick, "Transcending the Kafkaesque," *Critics, Monsters, Fanatics & Other Literary Essays*, Houghton Mifflin Harcourt Publishing Co., 2016. Originally published as "How Kafka Actually Lived," in the New Republic, April 11, 2014.

6. William Styron, "Auschwitz's Message," *New York Times*, June 25, 1974.

7. Cynthia Ozick, "A Liberal's Auschwitz," *The Pushcart Prize: First Edition*, 1976-7.

8. *Conversations with William Styron*, edited by James L.W. West. III, University of Mississippi Press, 1985.

9. Ibid.

10. Morris Dickstein, "The World in a Mirror: Problems of Distance in Recent American Fiction," *The Sewanee Review*, Summer 1981.

11. Cynthia Ozick, "Who Owns Anne Frank?" *The New Yorker*, October 6, 1997. Reprinted in Quarrel & Quandary, Alfred A, Knopf, 2000.

12. Cynthia Ozick, "All The World Wants The Jews Dead," *Esquire*, November 1974.
13. Cynthia Ozick, "Toward a New Yiddish," Judaism, Summer 1970. Reprinted in *Art & Ardor*, Alfred A. Knopf, 1983.
14. Cynthia Ozick, "All The World Wants The Jews Dead," *Esquire*, November 1970.
15. Joseph Lowin, "Cynthia Ozick," *Jewish Women: A Comprehensive Historical Encyclopedia*, March 20, 2009.
16. Tim Teicholz, Interview with Cynthia Ozick, "The Art of Fiction," Series (XCV), Paris Review 29, Spring 1987. Quoted in *Greek Mind/ Jewish Soul: The Conflicted Art of Cynthia Ozick*, by Victor Sandberg, University of Wisconsin Press, 1994.
17. Ibid.
18. Victor Sandberg, *Greek Mind/Jewish Soul: The Conflicted Art of Cynthia Ozick.*
19. Paul Morton, "An Interview With Cynthia Ozick," by Bookslut.com, December 2008.
20. Cynthia Ozick, "The Lessons of The Master," New York Review of Books, August 12, 1982. Reprinted in Art & Ardor, 1983.
21. Joseph Lowin, "Cynthia Ozick," Jewish Women: A Comprehensive Historical Encyclopedia, March 20, 2009.
22. "The Many Faces of Cynthia Ozick." Interview in The Atlantic, May 15, 1997.
23. Boris Kachka, "Cynthia Ozick Wants To Make A Few Pointed Distinctions About Writing, Feminism, and Politics," Vulture.com, July 5, 2016.
24. "The Many Faces of Cynthia Ozick," Interview in *The Atlantic*, May 15, 1997.
25. Francine Prose, "Idolatry in Miami," *New York Times Book Review*, September 10, 1989.
26. Emma Brockes, "A Life In Writing: Cynthia Ozick," *The Guardian*, July 4, 2011.
27. Joseph Lowin, "Cynthia Ozick," *Jewish Women: A Comprehensive Historical Encyclopedia*, March 20, 2009.
28. Cynthia Ozick, "Toward a New Yiddish," *Judaism*, 1970. Reprinted in *Art & Ardor*, Alfred A. Knopf, 1983.
29. Ibid.
30. Ibid.
31. Ibid.

CHAPTER 15 "WHO OWNS ANNE FRANK?"

1. Cynthia Ozick, "Who Owns Anne Frank?" *The New Yorker*, October 6, 1997. Reprinted in *Quarrel & Quandary*, Knopf, 2000.
2. Ibid.
3. Ibid. Rather than use Anne Frank's words taken from subsequent editions of the diary, as quoted by Ozick, I've quoted Anne's actual words as printed in the first American edition of *The Diary of a Young Girl*, published by Doubleday in 1952.
4. Bruno Bettelheim, "The Ignored Lesson of Anne Frank," *Harper's*, November 1960.
5. Cynthia Ozick, "Who Owns Anne Frank?" *The New Yorker*.
6. New research suggests that the Jews hiding in the Amsterdam attic might not have been betrayed by a paid informant. Rather, the research suggests that they were discovered by investigators who were looking for evidence of ration coupons that were forged and sold. They stumbled on the eight Jews in hiding and notified Nazi authorities. See "New Perspective on Anne Frank's Arrest," by Ronald Leopold, Executive Director, Anne Frank House. Published in December 2016.
7. Cynthia Ozick, "Who Owns Anne Frank?" *The New Yorker*.
8. Ibid.
9. Ibid.
10. Ibid.
11. Ibid.
12. Ibid.
13. Ibid.

CHAPTER 16 WHAT KIND OF JEW AM I?

1. Wolfgang Saxon, Obituary of Marshall Meyer, *New York Times*, December 31,1993.
2. Ibid.
3. Sandee Brawarsky, "A History of Congregation B'nai Jeshurun," www. bj.org.
4. Letty Cottin Pogrebin told me that she once invited Ozick, an Orthodox Jew, to services at B'nai Jeshurun. Ozick politely declined, saying she had been to services there before, calling the synagogue "the hootenanny on the Upper West Side."
5. Douglas Martin, "In His Despair, Rabbi's Strength Revives Temple,"

New York Times, October 3, 1987.

6. The congregation of B'nai Jeshurun left the Conservative movement in the 1990s and is now independent.

7. Rabbi Donniel Hartman, *Putting God Second: How To Save Religion From Itself*, Beacon Press, 2016.

8. In a subsequent interview, Sam Norich defined his own Judaism in this delightful way: "I would describe myself as a secular Jew, with qualifications... You know the [joke] about 'Goldberg goes to *shul* to talk to God. I go to shul to talk to Goldberg.' That's the kind of shul-goer I am. I'm not a believer, but I do think I should be. At least, I shouldn't proclaim my disbelief. Mainly because it would be an act of hubris."

9. "A Portrait of Jewish Americans," Pew Research Center, 2013. The survey estimated that there are 6.6 million Jews in America, or about 2.2% of the population. Of these, 5.3 million are adults and 1.3 million are children who are being raised at least partly as Jews. The Jewish population of Israel (estimated in 2015) is slightly larger: 6.7 million, according to the Israel Central Bureau of Statistics.

10. The Pew survey also shows that Reform Judaism continues to be the largest Jewish denomination in the U.S. (35% of all Jews), while 18% identify with Conservative Judaism, and 10% with Orthodox Judaism. (The proportion of Conservative Jews is much higher in the New York City area). Another 6% identify with other Jewish groups, such as the Reconstructionist and Jewish Renewal movements. The rest, about 31%, say they do not identify with any particular Jewish denomination.

11. Cited by Anne Roiphe, *Generation Without Memory: A Jewish Journey Through Christian America*, The Linden Press, 1981.

12. Irving Kristol, "The Future of American Jewry," *Commentary*, August 1991.

13. Lawrence Fuchs, *The American Kaleidoscope: Race, Ethnicity, and the Civic Culture*, Wesleyan University Press, 1990.

14. Various surveys cited by Richard L. Rubin measure the political attitudes of American Jews. See, for example, John C. Green, "American Religious Landscape and Political Attitudes, a Baseline for 2004," Fourth National Survey of Religion and Politics, Bliss Institute, University of Akron.

15. Jeremy Ben-Ami, "America's Jewish Vote," *New York Times*, November 12, 2012.

16. "Election 2016: Exit Polls," *New York Times*, updated from November 8, 2016.
17. The Torah, given by God to Moses on Mt. Sinai, describes Jewish history and law. The Talmud is detailed commentary on Jewish ritual and tradition, written by rabbis and scholars over the centuries.
18. Richard L. Rubin, *Jewish in America: Living George Washington's Promise*, Park International Publishing, 2016..
19. "A Portrait of Jewish Americans," Pew Research Center, 2013.
20. The concept of the chosen people dates to Abraham's covenant with God: Jews were chosen to spread monotheism throughout the world in exchange for the promised land of Israel.
21. "A Portrait of Jewish Americans," Pew Research Center, 2013.
22. Ibid.

EPILOGUE

1. See, for example, Bellow, by James Atlas, Random House, 2000. *The Life of Saul Bellow*, 1915-1964 by Zachary Leader, Alfred A. Knopf, 2015. *Bernard Malamud: A Writer's Life*, by Philip Davis, Oxford University Press, 2007. *Isaac Bashevis Singer: A Life*, by Janet Hadda, Oxford University Press, 1997. *Master of Dreams: A Memoir of Isaac Bashevis Singer*, Dvorah Telushkin, Perennial, 2004, and *Timebends: A Life*, by Arthur Miller, Grove Press, 1987.

Acknowledgements

Writing a book is an act of isolation. Once you've finished the reporting – or think you have – you sit in a room, alone with your thoughts and your Word doc. It's easy to take a wrong turn, hit a dead end, or get completely lost. Once you're done – or think you are – you need help.

In my case, Lynn Povich, was my guiding angel, as only a mate of 40 years can be. She read every chapter along the way, making many suggestions, enthusiastically telling me what passed muster, and gently letting me know where I had gone wrong. When I had finished the first draft, she had some further thoughts about the book's overall structure, a feat of literary engineering. Our children, Sarah and Ned, welcomed and enjoyed the personal musings of their father, but didn't have the same attachment to all the books that nurtured me. Why would they? I'm delighted they've developed their own literary tastes.

When I was ready to brave the outside world, I sent the manuscript to several friends. I'm grateful that they took the time to read the manuscript with such care and for their many thoughts, their candor, and their friendship. In alphabetical order, my thanks to Tim Harper, Michael Kinsley, Amy Kratka, Sam Norich, Peter Osnos, Letty Cottin Pogrebin, Fred Price, Victor Ripp, and Sammy Wasson.

Thanks also to Michael Kramer for encouraging me to pursue the idea when it was just a gleam in my eye, and to Amanda Urban for her wise counsel. And to Samuel Freedman, Bob Littell, and Celia McGee for their publishing guidance.

Finally, I'm grateful to Malcolm Frouman, the award-winning art director at *Business Week* when I was the editor, who designed the cover and the interior pages. And to Gabe Stuart of Bayberry Books and Kirsti Itameri of the CUNY Graduate School of Journalism, who took the manuscript and turned it into the small miracle of a published book.

Stephen B. Shepard
November 2017

About the Author

Stephen B. Shepard is the Founding Dean Emeritus of the Graduate School of Journalism at the City University of New York. He served as a senior editor at *Newsweek*, the editor of *Saturday Review*, and editor-in-chief of *Business Week*. From 1992 to 1994, he was president of the American Society of Magazine Editors. In addition to teaching at CUNY, Shepard was a faculty member at the Columbia Journalism School, where he was co-founder and first director of the Knight-Bagehot Fellowships, a mid-career program for working journalists. His book about journalism, *Deadlines and Disruption: My Turbulent Path From Print to Digital*, was published in 2012. He is married to Lynn Povich, author of *The Good Girls Revolt*, and they have two adult children.

Index

A

Acocella, Joan, 84
An American Type, 15
Anti-Defamation League, 101
The Adventures of Augie March,
    66, 77-82, 84-85, 92,
    115, 126
*The Adventures of Huckleberry
Finn,* 79, 83, 143
American Pastoral, 98, 114-115
Anti-Semitism, 23, 29, 37, 57,
    94, 95, 97, 100, 102, 110, 151,
    154, 157, 174
Assimilation, 15, 64, 68, 96,
    145, 157, 174, 177
The Assistant, 13, 115, 117, 120,
    123-127, 130
The Atlantic, 155
Auschwitz, 150-152, 154, 161-164
Auschwitz's Message, 150

B

Baldwin, James, 82
Bech: A Book, 138
Bech is Back, 138, 140

Bech at Bay, 138
Bellow, Saul, 13, 16, 65, 77-93
    94, 95, 102, 114, 126, 128,
    130, 149, 178, 180
  Book group discussion of,
    77-93
  Philip Roth's view of, 77-78
  His writing style, 84, 85
  Anti-Semitism directed
    at, 94, 95
  Reviews of *Augie March*,
    83-84
  Is *Herzog* a Jewish
    book? 92
  View of Bernard Mala-
    mud, 114-116
Bennington College, 129
Bergen-Belsen, 162, 165
Bildungsroman, 81, 84
Begley, Adam, 146
Bettelheim, Bruno, 161
Bigsby, Christopher, 56
Bloom, Claire, 126
B'nai Jeshurun, synagogue,
    168-171

Book group, 77, 81-82, 84, 129
Brandeis University, 174
Bread Givers, 16
Brooklyn Dodgers, 133-135
Bronstein, Marcelo, 171
Bloom, Harold, 140
Bloomgarden, Kermit, 164
Bradbury, Malcolm, 145
Broken Glass, 155
Brown, Ben, 41-43
Brown, Benjamin I. (Bib), 41
    43-47, 49-52
Brown, Don, 41, 47-52, 81, 87, 88, 91, 92
Brown, Esther, 44, 48-49
Bronx High School of Science, 12, 49
Brustein, Robert, 96
Buchenwald liberation, 20-21, 110
The Bulgarian Poetess, 138-139
Business Week, 22, 23, 27, 47

C
Cahan, Abraham, 15-16, 36, 61
Call it Sleep, 13, 14-15
The Cannibal Galaxy, 156
Capote, Truman, 95, 96
Chayefsky, Paddy, 102
Church of Saint Paul and Saint Andrew, 170, 171
City College of New York (CCNY), 12, 48-49, 61, 62, 64, 68, 71, 102, 119

Auditing a class at, 81
Jewish Studies Department, 61
Albert Einstein visit, 71
City University of New York Graduate School of Journalism, 14, 50, 64
Clarion agricultural colony, 42, 48
Utah, 42, 43, 48
Clinton, Hillary, 37, 175
Columbia University, 61
Commentary magazine, 54, 96, 115, 142
Couples, 106

D
Dangling Man, 77, 78, 95
Davis, Philip, 117, 118
Davis, Robert Gorham, 83
deChiara, Ann, 119-121
Death of a Salesman, 53-60
    Yiddish version, 54-55
Depression, the, 58-59, 119, 179
The Dean's December, 78
Defender of the Faith, 100
Dennehy, Brian, 59
The Diary of Anne Frank, 108, 160-166
The Diary of a Young Girl, 163
Dickstein, Morris, 128
Diversity, 81, 82
Doctorow, E.L., 13, 82, 178, 179

Dubin's Lives, 129, 130
Duke University, 154

E
Ehrenberg, Darlene, 55
Einstein, Albert, 71, 72
Eli, The Fanatic, 31-38, 110
Eliot, George, 82
Ellison, Ralph, 82, 103
Enemies, A Love Story, 66-67
Erasmus Hall High School, 119
The Executioner's Song, 99
Exit Ghost, 111-112, 117

F
The Facts, 99-101
Faulkner, William, 82
Fiedler, Leslie A., 14, 55, 56, 142
Fitzgerald, F. Scott, 82, 95
The Fixer, 115, 125, 127
Fo, Dario, 141
Focus, 57
Foreign Bodies, 156
The Forward, 10, 16, 81, 172
Frank, Anne, 108-111, 109, 152, 154, 160-166, 161, 164, 165, 166
Frank, Edith, 162
Frank, Margo, 162
Frank, Otto, 160-164
Freedman, Samuel, 62, 197
Freud, Sigmund, 173
Fuchs, Lawrence, 174

G
Gaddo, Frank, 142
Gansevoort Street, 39-41, 43, 44, 52, 59, 68, 81
Germany, first visit, 27-30
Gies, Miep, 162
Gilman, Richard, 96
Gimpel the Fool, 65, 79
The Ghost Writer, 99, 100, 106, 107, 109, 110, 151
Giroux, Robert, 121, 128
The Godfather, 105
God's Grace, 129
The Good Girls Revolt, 25, 198
Goodbye, Columbus, 33, 98, 100-102, 103, 105
Goodman, Teddy, 119
The Great Gatsby, 59, 99
The Guardian, 157

H
Hackett, Albert and Goodrich, Francis, 164
Hadda, Janet, 65, 66
Harcourt Brace, 121
Hart, Schaffner & Marx, 114
Hartman, Rabbi Donniel, 171
Hemingway, Ernest, 82, 95, 143
Heller, Joseph, 13, 178
Heller, Zoe, 149
Hellman, Lillian, 164
Henderson the Rain King, 78, 93
Herzog, 13, 77, 78, 88-92, 115
Heschel, Abraham Joshua, 175

Hinton, Mary Beth, 74
Hitler's bunker, 28, 29
Holocaust
    Concentration camps,
    150-152
    liberation of, 20, 110
    William Styron's view
    of, 150-152
    Cynthia Ozick's writing
    about it, 149, 151-159
    Anne Frank, death of, 162
Howe, Irving, 14, 102, 105
Hub Fans Bid Kid Adieu, 136
The Human Stain, 98
Humboldt's Gift, 78, 93
Hunter College High School,
    154

I
Incident at Vichy, 57
Invisible Man, 103
Israel, 32, 42, 48, 104, 170, 174,
    176

J
James, Henry, 95, 107, 155, 156
Joyce, James, 82
Jones, Judith, 138

K
Kafka, Franz, 150
Kafkaesque, 150
Kanin, Garson, 164
Kazin, Alfred, 14, 85, 102, 119,
    142

Kellman, Steven G., 15
Kibbutzim, 42, 48
Kingsbridge Heights Jewish
    Center, 18
Kolomaya, 27, 72, 73, 75
Kosner, Ed, 25
Kratka, Amy, 63, 64, 197
Kristol, Irving, 173
Kushner, Tony, 55

L
Leader, Zachary, 91
The Lesson of the Master, 155
Levi, Primo, 157
Library of America, 117
Lolita, 115
Luscher, Robert M., 144

M
Malamud, Bernard
    Early poverty, 118, 123,
    129, 179
    Mental illness in family,
    118
    Oregon years, 121
    The Assistant, "a master-
    piece," 115
    Work habits, 120
    Feud with Philip Roth, 10,
    125-127
    In Saul Bellow's shadow,
    128, 130-131
    The Magic Barrel, 115
Mailer, Norman, 96, 99, 126,
    144, 148, 158, 178

Mamet, David, 55
Masterpieces of Jewish Amer can Literature, 73
Matalon, Rolando, 170, 171
Mazursky, Paul, 67
Mencken, H.L., 158
Mercy of a Rude Stream, 15
Mercy, Pity, Peace, and Love, 155
The Messiah of Stockholm, 156
Meyer, Marshall, 168-170
MIT, 20, 71, 72
McCarthy, Mary, 56
Miller, Arthur, 10, 53-60, 149, 178, 179
Miller, Isidore, 57, 58, 59
Mittelman, Roy, 62
The Modern Jewish Canon, 127
The Modern Library, 106
Monroe, Marilyn, 58
Mount Vernon, NY, 48, 49
Mr. Sammler's Planet, 78, 93
My Father Is a Book, 116
My Life as a Man, 106

N
Nabokov, Vladimir, 115
The Naked and the Dead, 8
National Book Award, 77, 99, 102, 115, 128, 148, 151
The Natural, 115, 117, 119, 121-123, 130
Navasky, Victor, 81, 83, 87, 91
Nemesis, 98
A New Life, 116, 128

New Yiddish Rep, 55
New York Giants, 133
New York Yankees, 132-135
The New Yorker, 84, 99, 100, 137, 152, 156, 160
New York Daily News, 141, 165
The New York Times Book Review, 15, 83, 149
Newark Public Library, 102
Newsweek, 24, 25, 50
Nobel Prize in Literature, 16, 65, 77
Noon Wine, 95
Norich, Sam, 8, 81, 82, 87, 172
Novick, Julius, 56
NYU, Washington Square, 155

O
Oettinger, Marilyn Tanner, 27, 72, 75
Ohio State, 155
O'Malley, Walter, 134
O'Neill, Eugene, 54, 56
Oregon State College, 121
Orthodox Jews, 31, 32, 37, 38, 42, 177
Ozick, Cecilia and William, 152-153
Ozick, Cynthia, 10, 13, 63, 117, 128,143, 144, 148-158, 160, 162, 163, 164, 165-167, 169, 177

P

Paley, Grace, 13, 178
Partisan Review, 115, 142, 145
Pew Research Center,
    "A Portrait of Jewish
    Americans, 2013," 172
Pierpont, Claudia Roth, 99,
    106
Pinsker, Sanford, 144
Pluenneke, Jack, 27
Podhoretz, Norman, 105, 142
Pogrebin, Bert, 81, 87, 90, 129
Pogrebin, Letty Cottin, 130,
    197
Portman, Natalie, 165
Portnoy's Complaint, 98, 99,
    106, 115
Pound, Ezra, 95
Porter, Katherine Anne, 95, 97
Povich, Ethyl Friedman, 25, 26
Povich, Lynn, 24, 26, 27, 29,
    167, 168, 171,172, 196
Povich, Shirley, 26-27
*Prisoner Without a Name, Cell
    Without a Number*, 169
Pritchett, V.S., 85
Priven, Ari, 170, 171
Proust, Marcel, 158
Pulitzer Prize, 99, 114, 115,
    128, 148, 165, 180
*Putting God Second: How to
    Save Religion From Itself*,
    171
Pynchon, Thomas, 141

R

Rabbit novels, 135, 139, 145-147
Radcliffe College, 22, 49, 89, 101
Ravelstein, 77
The Rise of David Levinsky,
    15, 36
Robinson, Jackie, 133
Rodeph Shalom synagogue, 168
Rosen, Jonathan, 125
Rosenberg, Julius and Ethel, 21
Roosevelt, Eleanor, 163
Roosevelt, NJ, 64
Rosenthal, Jack, 81, 82, 84, 85, 92,
    186
Ross, George, 54
Ross, Michael, 62
Rothberg, Michael, 102, 110
Roth, Henry, 14, 15, 61, 102,
    137
Roth, Philip,
    Criticized by Jews, 101,
    103-106
    Nathan Zuckerman, 99,
    100, 107-109, 110-113
    alter ego, 99, 100
    Maggie Williams, first
    wife, 103, 106
    Portnoy fallout, 104-106
    Re-imagining Anne
    Frank, 109
    On Saul Bellow, 77-78
    Feud with Bernard
    Malamud, 10, 125-127
    Retirement, 113
Roth Unbound, 99

Rubin, Richard R., 175
Rutgers University, Newark
    campus, 102

S
Sabbath's Theater, 98
Sage, Martin, 81, 86
Salinger, J.D., 9, 13, 136, 137,
    143, 178
Satan in Goray, 66
Schindler's List, 29
The Secret Annex, 163
Seize the Day, 77, 78, 85-88, 92
Shapiro, William, 18
The Shawl, 156, 157
Shaw, Peter, 105
Shep, 40, 41, 45, 46, 47, 48, 49,
    50, 52, 53, 54, 59
Shepard, Ned, 72, 171, 196
Shepard, Ruth Tanner, 12, 16,
    19, 21, 27, 46,50, 70, 73, 74,
    75
Shepard, Sarah, 29, 134, 168,
    170, 171, 196
Shepard, William (Shep),
    17-18, 20, 27, 40, 41, 44, 45,
    46, 47, 48, 49, 50, 52, 53, 54,
    59
Shepard, Stephen B.,
    Parents' Jewish identity, 17-
    22, 26-27, 29-30
    At CCNY, 49
    Encountering anti-Semi
    tism, 62
    First wife, 22-24
    Jewish life with Lynn
    Povich, 26-27, 171-172
    As secular Jew, 170, 171,
    172, 173, 175, 176, 177
Ship of Fools, 95
Shop Talk, 77
Short Friday, 65
Simon, John, 96, 141
Singer, Isaac Bashevis, 13,
    61-69
Slattery, Mary Grace, 58
Smith, Janna Malamud, 116,
    118, 129
Sol, Felicia, 170
Sophie's Choice, 151, 152
Spielberg, Steven, 29
The Spinoza of Market Street,
    65
Stage Delicatessen, 103
Sternlicht, Sanford, 27, 73-75
Sternlicht, Bobbie, 73, 75
Strandberg, Victor, 154
Straus, Roger, 130
Strasberg, Susan, 164
Streep, Meryl, 152
Styron, William, 150-152
Suwalki, 27
Swados, Harvey, 116
Syracuse University, 73

T
Talumud, 33
Tanenzapf, Benjamin, 70, 72,
    73, 75
Tanenzapf, Bella, 75

Tanenzapf, Millie Zwilich, 72, 73, 75
Tanner, Lou, 20, 71, 72
Tanner, Ruth, 19, 70, 73, 75
Teitelbaum, Herb, 81, 83, 86, 87, 92
Telushkin, Dvorah, 65
The Tenants, 128
The Tenement Saga: The Lower East Side and Early Jewish American Writers, 73
Tikkun olam, 175
Time magazine, 25, 106, 115, 142
Timebends, 57-59
Timerman, Jacobo, 169
Toward a New Yiddish, 157
Townsend Harris High School, 71, 72
Trump, Donald, 37, 174-176
Trust, 148, 155
Twain, Mark, 82, 143
Tzedakah, 175

U
UJA-Federation of New York, 31
Updike, John, 106, 135, 136, 137, 138-147, 150
Uris, Leon, 102

V
Van Daan, Peter, 161, 164
Variety, 164
Vassar College, 25

The Victim, 78, 92
Vidal, Gore, 95-97

W
Washington Post, 26
The White Negro, 126
Weissmandl, Michael, 36
"*Who Owns Anne Frank?*," 160
Wiesel, Elie, 157
Williams, Tennessee, 56
Willis, Jack, 81, 82
Wilson, Edmund, 95
Wilson, August, 56
Wisse, Ruth, 127, 128
Woolf, Virginia, 82
World of Our Fathers, 14
Wright, Richard, 82

Y
Yeshiva University, 103, 108, 110
Yezierska, Anzia, 16

Z
Zuckerman Bound, 117

Made in the USA
Middletown, DE
03 May 2018